新SAT
文法真经总纲

曲萌 编著

中国人民大学出版社
·北京·

图书在版编目(CIP)数据

SAT文法真经总纲 / 曲萌编著. —北京：中国人民大学出版社，2020.7
ISBN 978-7-300-28229-9

Ⅰ.①S… Ⅱ.①曲… Ⅲ.①英语-语法-高等学校-入学考试-美国-自学参考资料 Ⅳ.①H314

中国版本图书馆CIP数据核字（2020）第105279号

- 本书中所有理论、概念均系作者原创，如果引用需注明出处。
- 本书著作权归作者所有，版权归中国人民大学出版社，任何复印、引用均需征求著作权人及版权持有人同时同意。

SAT文法真经总纲

曲萌　编著

SAT Wenfa Zhenjing Zonggang

出版发行	中国人民大学出版社			
社　　址	北京中关村大街31号		邮政编码	100080
电　　话	010-62511242（总编室）		010-62511770（质管部）	
	010-82501766（邮购部）		010-62514148（门市部）	
	010-62515195（发行公司）		010-62515275（盗版举报）	
网　　址	http://www.crup.com.cn			
	http://www.1kao.com.cn（中国1考网）			
经　　销	新华书店			
印　　刷	北京玺诚印务有限公司			
规　　格	170mm×230mm　16开本		版　次	2020年7月第1版
印　　张	11　插页1		印　次	2020年7月第1次印刷
字　　数	122 000		定　价	29.00元

封面无防伪标均为盗版

版权所有　　侵权必究　　印装差错　　负责调换

序 言

SAT 考试改革之后，SAT 语法考试改成 SAT 文法考试，不仅把单独的语法题目嵌进文章内容中进行考查，还增添了对文章中心思想及作者表达观点的理解能力的考查。耳目一新的考试形式，给考生们带来新鲜感的同时，也增加了新的考试难度，对考生提出了新的要求，比如阅读理解速度的提升、对文章观点的精准把握等。

不过，考生们不要担心，这本《SAT 文法真经总纲》覆盖了 SAT 文法考试的全部难点，忧考生之忧，解考生之难。首先，这本书在第二章中针对考生们最头疼的 SAT 长难句进行了分析讲解，若具备了书中讲解的长难句删减方法，考生们就会犹如佩戴了一副透视眼镜，一秒看清句子主干结构，再也不会因为阅读速度慢、答不完题而困扰了。其次，在第三章和第四章中针对 SAT 文法考试两大类型题即观点表达类题目和标准语法类题目进行了技巧讲解，28 种题型的解题技巧真经将带领考生们一路过关斩将，朝 SAT 文法满分的目的地挺进。最后，在第五章到第八章中针对四种文章体裁，对四篇 SAT 文法考试的文章及真题进行了真经派的细致讲解，对真经理论的运用与实践会让考生们拨开 SAT 文法考试的迷雾，看见明媚的阳光。

希望这本《SAT 文法真经总纲》能陪伴考生们踏上努力奋斗的留学之路，为这条艰辛之路带来一丝轻松，让考生们事半功倍，一路向前。

致谢：

感谢考生们，你们不断的敦促和鼓励，让我以前所未有的热情和执着完成这本书。

感谢刘洪波老师、吕蕾老师在本书的编写中给予我的宝贵意见。

特别感谢美文苑公司与学为贵教育集团为本书出版提供的大力支持。

曲萌微信号： mengkerryqu

曲萌新浪微博： @曲萌_学为贵

目 录

第一章　洞察SAT文法考试 /1

　　一、考试特点 /2

　　二、考查技能 /3

　　三、题型分类 /4

第二章　SAT长难句分析 /7

　　一、长难句分析讲解 /8

　　二、篇章长难句删减训练 /16

第三章　观点表达类题目（Expression of Ideas）技巧真经 /27

　　一、文章发展题（Development）/28

　　二、文章结构题（Organization）/41

　　三、有效词句运用题（Effective Language Use）/55

第四章　标准语法类题目（Standard English Conventions）技巧真经 /65

　　一、句子结构题（Sentence Structure）/66

　　二、标准用法题（Conventions of Usage）/81

　　三、标准符号题（Conventions of Punctuation）/101

第五章　历史/社会研究类文章真题精讲 /113

第六章　科学类文章真题精讲 /127

第七章　职业类文章真题精讲 /141

第八章　人文学科类文章真题精讲 /155

第一章

洞察SAT文法考试

一、考试特点

首先，我们了解一下 SAT 考试的构成：

考试内容	考试时间（分钟）	题目数量
Reading	65	52
Writing and Language	35	44
Math	80	58
Essay (optional)	50	1
Total	180 (230 with Essay)	154 (155 with Essay)

如上图所示，SAT 考试分为四个部分，其中第四部分 Essay（短文写作）是选考。

接下来，我们看看 SAT 文法考试的具体特点：

题量： 44 道单选题。

总时长： 35 分钟（平均每道题用时不到 1 分钟）。

文章数量： 4 篇。

文章长度： 400～450 词/篇。

文章主题： 4 篇文章分别涉及职业、人文学科、社会/历史研究和科学。

文章体裁： 1 篇非小说类记叙文；1～2 篇说明文；1～2 篇议论文。

注意： 答错题不会被扣分！

二、考查技能

官方申明：在文法考试中强调四大技能：Expression of Ideals（观点的表达）、Standard English Conventions（标准语法）、Command of Evidence（对证据的掌控）和 Words in Context（语境中的词义）。

★ *Expression of Ideals*（观点的表达）

该能力测试体现在 SAT 文法考试中，包含两个方面：

● 修正文章内容以达成文章的目的。

● 提升文章结构，强化文章逻辑。

★ *Standard English Conventions*（标准语法）

该能力测试体现在 SAT 文法考试中，包含三个方面：

● 修正句子结构与形式。

● 掌握语法中动词、代词、名词、所有格和固定搭配的用法。

● 正确掌握标点符号的用法。

★ *Command of Evidence*（对证据的掌控）

该能力测试体现在 SAT 文法考试中，包含三个方面：

- 修正对于图表信息做出的错误的数据解读。

- 添加或修正观点以提升文章清晰度。

- 添加或修正具体描述或举例以提升文章观点。

★ Words in Context（语境中的词义）

该能力测试体现在 SAT 文法考试中，包含三个方面：

- 用简洁表达替代冗长多余的表达。

- 精确用词表达文章观点。

- 选用符合文章写作风格的词汇。

三、题型分类

虽然 SAT 文法考试的所有题目都是单选题，看上去形式一致，但实际上每道题的测试考点和命题目的都是不同的。

根据《最新 SAT 考试官方指南》，44 道选择题可分为两大类，共 28 种题型：

A. 观点表达类题目（Expression of Ideas）

★ 文章发展题（Development）

① 主旨题 (Proposition)

② 论据题 (Support)

③ 焦点题 (Focus)

④ 数据信息题 (Quantitative information)

★ 文章结构题（*Organization*）

① 逻辑顺序题 (Logical sequence)

② 开篇句 & 结论句 & 过渡句题 (Introductions, conclusions, and transitions)

★ 有效词句运用题（*Effective Language Use*）

① 措辞题 (Precision)

② 简洁性题 (Concision)

③ 风格 & 语气题 (Style and tone)

④ 句法题 (Syntax)

B. 标准语法类题目（Standard English Conventions）

★ 句子结构题（*Sentence Structure*）

① 句子边界题 (Sentence boundaries)

② 从属连词和并列连词题 (Subordination and coordination)

③ 平行结构题 (Parallel structure)

④ 悬垂修饰语题 (Modifier placement)

⑤ 时态题 (Shifts in verb tense, mode, and voice)

⑥ 人称混淆题 (Shifts in pronoun person and number)

★ 标准用法题（*Conventions of Usage*）

① 指代题 (Pronoun clarity)

② 所有格题 (Possessive determiners)

③ 一致性题 (Agreement)

④ 易混词题 (Frequently confused words)

⑤ 比较结构题 (Logical comparison)

⑥ 标准搭配题 (Conventional expression)

★ 标准符号题（*Conventions of Punctuation*）

① 句末符号题 (End-of-sentence punctuation)

② 句中符号题 (Within-sentence punctuation)

③ 名词所有格 & 代词所有格题 (Possessive nouns and pronouns)

④ 并列符号题 (Items in a series)

⑤ 插入符号题 (Nonrestrictive and parenthetical elements)

⑥ 多余符号题 (Unnecessary punctuation)

以上两大类共 28 种题型的解题技巧真经，将在第三章和第四章逐一详细讲解。请考生们务必认真学习掌握。

第二章

SAT长难句分析

一、长难句分析讲解

　　SAT 考试改革后，SAT 文法考试就不再是单纯考查语法知识的考试了，所有的文法题目都嵌在文章中，另外还添加了考查文章观点和文章结构的题目；并且，考试时间只有 35 分钟，要完成 4 篇文章 44 道题，平均每道题的解题时间不足 1 分钟，这些变化都要求考生们有更强的阅读能力和更快的阅读速度，所以对 SAT 长难句的把握和理解就显得格外重要。如何能迅速分辨长难句的主谓宾结构呢？下面我将通过 12 组长难句的分析为考生们解密。

★ 长难句分析 1

> I suggest transforming our social system from a bureaucratically managed industrialism in which maximal production and consumption are ends in themselves into a humanist industrialism in which man and full development of his potentialities—those of love and of reason—are the aims of all social arrangements.

分析： 大家可能不知道，英语中有很多词对，它们就像 couple 一样，永远是成对地出现，比如 "from…to…" "so…that…" "such…as…" "between…and" "too…to…" 等，所以大家要对这些词对极其敏锐，看到其中一个，就想到另一个，这样句子顿时就变得简单明了。在上面的句子中，我们就看到一对 "from…into…"，这样句子就可以直接简化成 "I suggest transforming our social system from…into…"。大家是不是豁然开朗？另外，我们还看到 from 和 into 后面的 industrialism 之后都跟着 in which 结构，很明显都引导定语从句，只起到修饰作用，所以可以直接删减。那么，这个句子就变成了 "I suggest transforming our social system from a bureaucratically managed industrialism into a humanist industrialism."，句意是：我建议把我们的社会体系从一个官僚主义管理的工业制度变成一个人道主义的工业制度。这样一来，长难句是不是就变得简单了？

★ 长难句分析 2

> Some of the most significant finds have involved complete mammoth carcasses preserved in the glaciers and permafrost of Siberia and Alaska, which are particularly useful to scientists because they provide samples of tissue, hair, and even undigested food from these creatures that perished so long ago.

分析：英语中修饰语成分很多，这些修饰语在句子中只是起到修饰名词的作用，所以将其删去也不会影响句子的完整性。修饰语成分包括形容词、定语从句、介词短语和非谓语动词，考生们如果看到句子中有这些成分，是可以直接删除的。下面，我们来分析一下这个句子，这个句子被逗号隔开了前后半句，后半句很明显是 which 引导的定语从句，所以可删，那么主句肯定出现在前半句中；主句的主语应该是 finds，finds 在句中作名词，前面的 some of the most significant 都是 finds 的前置定语，谓语动词是 have involved，宾语是 mammoth carcasses（猛犸象的尸体），preserved 则是放在名词 carcasses 后面的非谓语动词作后置定语，所以也可以删除。这样句子的主干就明确了，是 "finds have involved mammoth carcasses"，可翻译为 "发现中涉及很多猛犸象的尸体"，这就是作者最想表达的内容。

★ 长难句分析 3

> Estimates indicate that the aquifer contains enough water to fill Lake Huron, but unfortunately, under the semiarid climatic conditions that presently exist in the region, rates of addition to the aquifer are minimal, amounting to about half a centimeter a year.

分析：长难句之所以长，是因为大部分的句子有连词，比如并列连词 and、转折连词 but、yet、while、whereas 等。这些连词的出现，意味着这个句子不仅仅有一个主干。在这个句子中，我们就看到了一个转折连词 but，所以大家应该清楚的是 but 前后会各有一个主谓宾结构。前面的句子主语是 estimates，谓语是 indicate，后面跟了一个 that 引导的宾语从句，而宾语从句在主谓宾结构中起到实体作用，不能删，所以第一个句子的主干是 "Estimates indicate that the aquifer contains enough water"；连词 but 后面的句子中，"under…region" 作状语，可以删除，"amounting to…a year" 作伴随状语，也可以删除，所以后面句子的主干是 "rates of addition to the aquifer are minimal"。整个句子提取主干的结果是：Estimates indicate that the aquifer contains enough water, but rates of addition to the aquifer are minimal. 句意是：估计表明蓄水层含有足够的水，但是水增加的比率是很小的。

★ 长难句分析 4

> The same dramatic technological changes that have provided marketers with more communications choices have also increased the risk that passionate consumers will voice their opinions in quicker, more visible and much more damaging ways.

分析：在英语中我们学过很多从句，在分析长难句时，定语从句、状语从句和同位语从句都属于我们要删去的内容，因为定语从句修饰名词，起到形容词的作用，而状语从句对句子的主谓宾结构起到补充作用，所以都可以删去。在上面的句子中，我们看到了两个由 that 引导的从句，这两个从句都跟在名词后面，但是这两个从句并不一样，changes 后面的从句是定语从句，而 risk 后面的从句是同位语从句。大家知道为什么吗？定语从句最大的特点是句子不完整，而同位语从句却是完整的，这是我们区分同位语从句和定语从句的根本。所以这个句子的主谓宾就是 "technological changes have increased the risk"，意思是 "技术变化增加了风险"。

★ 长难句分析 5

> Because this water cannot drain down through the solid permafrost, it collects at the surface, forming bogs and ponds that provide water for the survival of both plants and animals and even act as breeding grounds for some insects.

分析：在长难句中，大家经常会看到许多双逗号（即两个逗号隔开一段内容），这往往是插入语的标志。很多人对此产生了错误印象，误认为只要看到双逗号，就可以把它们之间的内容删掉，但是经常遇到的情况是删掉双逗号之间的内容后，这句话的谓语动词也被删掉了。这是怎么回事呢？其实是大家对双逗号的理解存在问题，只有当双逗号中间是单词、词组或从句时，中间的内容才是插入语，可删；如果双逗号中间是句子，就不能进行删除了，因为它恰恰就是句子的主干。就如上面这个句子，我们看到了一个双逗号，如果像以前那样认为中间部分是插入语，把它删掉，那么本句只剩下一个 because 引导的原因状语从句和一个分词 forming 引出的伴随状语，这句话就没有主句了，所以不能删减双逗号之间的内容。在这个句子中，双逗号之间是一个完整句子，也就是这句话的主干 "it collects at the surface"，而 it 在原文中指代 water，所以主干可翻译成：水在表面汇集。

★ 长难句分析 6

> Washington, who had begun to believe that all men were created equal after observing the bravery of the black soldiers during the Revolutionary War, overcame the strong opposition of his relatives to grant his slaves their freedom in his will.

分析：我们再来复习一下双逗号的知识，在这个句子中双逗号之间的内容是 who 引导的一个定语从句，我之前跟大家说过，当双逗号之间是单词、词组或从句时，它们之间的内容是可以直接删减的，剩下的部分即为句子的主干结构。本句的主句是：Washington overcame the strong opposition of his relatives to grant his slaves their freedom in his will. 大家在翻译这句话的时候需要注意三个词：opposition 是"反对"的意思，用法是 opposition to；grant 是"给予"的意思；will 在这里作名词，应翻译成"遗嘱"的意思。所以这句话的意思是：华盛顿克服了亲戚们的强烈反对，在遗嘱中给予他的奴隶自由。

★ 长难句分析 7

> Though it may be difficult to imagine from a later perspective, a strain of critical opinion in the 1920s predicted that sound film would be a technical novelty that would soon fade from sight, just as had many previous attempts, dating well back before the First World War, to link images with recorded sound.

分析：此句无论从句法结构还是从句意理解上看，难度都很大，句法结构难是因为此句中包含了很多的句法成分，句意理解难是因为句中有很多词在人们的理解中都存在偏差。句中有三个双逗号，我们先来分析双逗号之间的成分：第一个双逗号之间的 a strain of critical opinion 是主语，predicted 是谓语，that 引导了宾语从句，所以第一个双逗号之间的内容是句子，所以不能删；第二个双逗号之间是 just as 引导的方式状语，可删；第三个双逗号中间是现在分词 dating 作 attempts 的后置定语，也可以删掉。而余下的部分中，though 引导让步状语从句，可以删，to link 作目的状语，可以删，所以本句的主干是 "a strain of critical opinion in the 1920s predicted that sound film would be a technical novelty that would soon fade from sight"。需要注意的词有 a strain of，是"一系列"的意思，novelty 是名词，意思是"创新"，fade from sight 的意思是"从视野中消失"，所以主干可翻译成：20 世纪 20 年代的一系列批判的观点预言有声电影会是一个技术上的创新，但很快会从视野中消失。

长难句分析 8

As a result of crustal adjustments and faulting, the Strait of Gibraltar, where the Mediterranean now connects to the Atlantic, opened, and water cascaded spectacularly back into the Mediterranean.

分析：此句的复杂性在于里面的逗号过多，很多考生看到如此多的逗号就会发蒙，而且在试图采用双逗号的技巧来进行删减时，会发现仍然存在问题。很多考生都忽略了句中有一个并列连词 and，并列连词可以连接并列的单词、词组和句子，只要句中存在并列连词，大家一定要看清它的并列成分，这样才能进一步分析。那如何看清前后并列的成分呢？其实，在看连词的时候也是有顺序原则的，一般先看连词后面的成分，然后向前推导与其并列的成分。我们来实践一下，该句 and 后面的 water 是主语，cascaded 是动词作谓语，很明显构成了一个句子，那就说明 and 前面也应该有一个与其并列的句子，所以这个长句有两个主干。接下来我们再分析一下 and 前面的句子成分，as a result of 引导的是原因状语，可以删掉，where 引导的定语从句在双逗号之间，也可以删掉，剩下的部分中 the Strait of Gibraltar 是主语，opened 是谓语动词。整理一下，可知句子主干是 "the Strait of Gibraltar opened and water cascaded back into the Mediterranean"，意思是：直布罗陀海峡打开，水就涌回了地中海。

长难句分析 9

Most engravings, for example, are best lit from the left, as befits the work of right-handed artists, who generally prefer to have the light source on the left so that the shadow of their hand does not fall on the tip of the engraving tool or brush.

分析：考生们在删减这个句子的时候，有一个部分比较容易确认，即 who 引导的定语从句，修饰 artists；而对于 as befits the work of right-handed artists 这部分，很多考生会比较迷惑，不清楚 as 在这里引导的是什么从句，是什么意思。as 这个词很小，但是词义却很多，如果对它的用法不清楚，就会对很多长难句产生理解误差，所以下面我们就来讲一下。当 as 后面跟名词或名词短语的时候，它的意思是"作为"；当 as 后面接句子时，它会有"因为""当""正如"这三个意思；当 as 后面跟不完整句子的时候，它相当于 which，引导非限定性定语从句。了解了这些，我们再看这个句子，as 后面跟的应该是一个不完整的句子，缺少一个主语，所以 as 在这里相当于 which，引导的是定语从句，所以也可以删掉。那么，这个句子的主干就是"most engravings are best lit from the left"，注意 lit 这个词，它是 light 的过去分词，light 作动词是"照亮"的意思，所以此句可翻译成：大部分的雕刻都是从左边照亮的。

★ 长难句分析 10

> It is significant that the earliest living things that built communities on these islands are examples of symbiosis, a phenomenon that depends upon the close cooperation of two or more forms of life and a principle that is very important in island communities.

分析：在分析这个句子时，我们看到句中有一个逗号。标点符号在句子中起着至关重要的作用，但是很多考生往往会忽略这一点，下面我就讲讲常用的一些标点符号的作用：逗号在句子中可以连接并列的单词、词组或从句，但是不能连接并列的句子；分号可以连接并列的句子，作用相当于连词；冒号和破折号后面可以跟词或者句子，引导同位语。所以当我们看到句子中只有一个逗号的时候，我们知道逗号不可以连接并列的句子，所以两个句子中肯定有一个是主句，另外一个则是可以删减的部分。很明显，在这个句子中，逗号后面是 a phenomenon and a principle 的并列，并列的是两个单词，所以可以删减。那么，逗号后面的内容是什么成分呢？大家注意一个句式："S（主语）+V（谓语）+O（宾语），（也可以用：或—）+noun"，也就是主谓宾完整的句子后面跟逗号或冒号或破折号再跟一个名词，这个名词就叫作同位语，用来解释前面的宾语。在这个句子里 a phenomenon and a principle 是 symbiosis

的同位语，可以删去。所以本句的主句在逗号前面，同时，逗号前面的句子里还存在一个定语从句 that built communities on these islands，可以删。那么，本句的主干就是 "it is significant that the earliest living things are examples of symbiosis"，可翻译为：最早期的生物都是共生关系的范例，这一点具有重大意义。

★ 长难句分析 11

Unlike in the Americas, where metallurgy was a very late and limited development, Africans had iron from a relatively early date, developing ingenious furnaces to produce the high heat needed for production and to control the amount of air that reached the carbon and iron ore necessary for making iron.

分析：本句考查的还是双逗号的删减技巧。第一个双逗号之间是 where 引导的定语从句修饰 Americas，可以删；第二个双逗号之间是一个句子，所以需要保留，而且基本可以确定这就是本句主干，那么其他部分都可以删除。那 developing 引导的是什么成分呢？我们来讲解一下：在 "S + V + O, v.-ing/v.-ed..." 或者 "v.-ing/v.-ed..., S + V + O" 的结构中，也就是在主谓宾结构的句子前后出现的分词引导的部分，我们统一叫作伴随状语。伴随状语的意思就是主语在发生主句动作的同时也在发生伴随的动作，所以分词的逻辑主语需要看主句的主语，本句中 developing 的逻辑主语是 Africans。那么，本句的主干就是 "Africans had iron from a relatively early date"，即非洲人在很早的时候就有铁了。

★ 长难句分析 12

Contrary to the arguments of some that much of the pacific was settled by Polynesians accidentally marooned after being lost and adrift, it seems reasonable that this feat was accomplished by deliberate colonization expeditions that set out fully stocked with food and domesticated plants and animals.

分析：本句中只有一个逗号，所以逗号隔开的两个部分中一个是主句，另一个的成分则可删。很明显，"Contrary to..."作的是比较状语，句子主干应该是"it seems reasonable that..."，句末的 that set out fully stocked with food and domesticated plants and animals 是定语从句，也可以删除。很多人会问：主句"it seems reasonable that..."是什么句型？考生们请注意，这个主句中的 it 不是代词，而是形式主语，真正的主语是 that 后面的部分，所以这个句型是主语从句的变形，正常的写法应该是 that this feat was accomplished by deliberate colonization expeditions that set out fully stocked with food and domesticated plants and animals seems reasonable，但如果这样写会显得头重脚轻，所以才把主语从句的内容都甩到了后面。主语从句变形的句型还有"it seems/appears that..." "it is + *adj./n./v.*-ed that..."等，考生们看到这样的句型，在翻译时要把 that 部分内容放在前面，也就是把句子还原成主语从句的模式再进行翻译。另外，这个主句里出现了 this feat，当句中出现代词有指代的时候，考生们一定要到前文中把指代弄清楚再翻译此句，这样句子才能翻译得明白。this feat 指的是前文的 much of the Pacific was settled by Polynesians，那么，句子主干的意思是：在太平洋大部分地区定居这一壮举是由深思熟虑的殖民探险队完成的这种说法似乎更合理。

二、篇章长难句删减训练

★ 自我检测 1

Librarians Help Navigate in the Digital Age

In recent years, public libraries in the United States have experienced reductions in their operating funds due to cuts imposed at the federal, state, and local government levels. Consequently, library staffing has been cut by almost four percent since 2008, and the demand for librarians continues to decrease, even though half of public libraries report that they have an insufficient number of staff to meet their patrons' needs.

Employment in all job sectors in the United States is projected to grow by fourteen percent over the next decade, yet the expected growth rate for librarians is predicted to be only seven percent, or half of the overall rate. This trend, combined with the increasing accessibility of information via the Internet, has led some to claim that librarianship is in decline as a profession. As public libraries adapt to rapid technological advances in information distribution, librarians' roles are actually expanding.

The share of library materials that is in non-print formats is increasing steadily; in 2010, at least 18.5 million e-books were available for circulation. As a result, librarians must now be proficient curators of electronic information, compiling, cataloging, and updating these collections. But perhaps even more importantly, librarians function as first responders for their communities' computer needs. Since one of the fastest growing library services is public access computer use, there is great demand for computer instruction. In fact, many librarians, whose training now includes courses on research and Internet search methods, teach classes in Internet navigation, database and software use, and digital information literacy. While these classes are particularly helpful to young students developing basic research skills, adult patrons can also benefit from librarian assistance in that they can acquire job-relevant computer skills. During periods of economic recession, public libraries and librarians are especially valuable, because they offer free resources that may be difficult to find elsewhere, such as help with online job searches as well as résumé and job material development. An overwhelming number of public libraries also report that they provide help with electronic government resources related to income taxes, legal issues, and retirement programs. In sum, the Internet does not replace the need for librarians, and librarians are hardly obsolete. The growth of electronic information has led to a diversification of librarians' skills and services, positioning them as savvy resource specialists for patrons.

★ 自我检测 1 删减答案

Librarians Help Navigate in the Digital Age

<u>In recent years (时间状语)</u>, public libraries in the United States have experienced reductions

in their operating funds due to cuts imposed at the federal, state, and local government levels（原因状语）. Consequently, library staffing has been cut by almost four percent since 2008, and the demand for librarians continues to decrease, even though half of public libraries report that they have an insufficient number of staff to meet their patrons' needs（让步状语从句）.

Employment in all job sectors in the United States is projected to grow by fourteen percent over the next decade, yet the expected growth rate for librarians is predicted to be only seven percent, or half of the overall rate. This trend, combined with the increasing accessibility of information via the Internet（插入语）, has led some to claim that librarianship is in decline as a profession. As public libraries adapt to rapid technological advances in information distribution（伴随状语）, librarians' roles are actually expanding.

The share of library materials that is in non-print formats（定语从句） is increasing steadily; in 2010, at least 18.5 million e-books were available for circulation. As a result, librarians must now be proficient curators of electronic information, compiling, cataloging, and updating these collections. But perhaps even more importantly, librarians function as first responders for their communities' computer needs. Since one of the fastest growing library services is public access computer use（原因状语从句）, there is great demand for computer instruction. In fact, many librarians, whose training now includes courses on research and Internet search methods（定语从句）, teach classes in Internet navigation, database and software use, and digital information literacy. While these classes are particularly helpful to young students developing basic research skills（让步状语从句）, adult patrons can also benefit from librarian assistance in that they can acquire job-relevant computer skills. During periods of economic recession（时间状语）, public libraries and librarians are especially valuable, because they offer free resources that may be difficult to find elsewhere, such as help with online job searches as well as résumé and job material development（原因状语从句）. An overwhelming number of public libraries also report that they provide help with electronic government resources related to income taxes, legal issues, and retirement programs（后置定语）. In sum, the Internet does not replace the need for librarians, and librarians are hardly obsolete. The growth of electronic information has led to a diversification of librarians' skills and services, <u>positioning them as savvy resource specialists for patrons（伴随状语）</u>.

⭐ 自我检测 2

A Quick Fix in a Throwaway Culture

Planned obsolescence, a practice whereby products are designed to have a limited period of usefulness, has been a cornerstone of manufacturing strategy for the past 80 years. This approach increases sales, but it also stands in stark contrast to a time when goods were produced to be durable. Planned obsolescence wastes materials as well as energy in making and shipping new products. It also reinforces the belief that it is easier to replace goods than to mend them, as repair shops are rare and repair methods are often specialized. In 2009, an enterprising movement, the Repair Café, challenged this widely accepted belief.

More like a fair than an actual café, the first Repair Café took place in Amsterdam, the Netherlands. It was the brainchild of former journalist Martine Postma, who wanted to take a practical stand in a throwaway culture. Her goals were straightforward: reduce waste, maintain and perpetuate knowledge and skills, and strengthen community. Since the inaugural Repair Café, others have been hosted in theater foyers, community centers, hotels, and auditoriums. Participants bring all manner of damaged articles—clothing, appliances, furniture, and more—to be repaired by a staff of volunteer specialists including tailors, electricians, and carpenters. While awaiting for service, patrons can enjoy coffee and snacks and mingle with their neighbors in need.

Though only about 3 percent of the Netherlands' municipal waste ends up in landfills, Repair Cafés still raise awareness about what may otherwise be mindless acts of waste by providing a venue for people to share and learn valuable skills that are in danger of being lost. It is easy to classify old but fixable items as "junk" in an era that places great emphasis on the next big thing. In helping people consider how the goods they use on a daily basis work and are made, Repair Cafés restore a sense of relationship between human beings and material goods.

Though the concept remained a local trend at first, international Repair Cafés, all affiliated with the Dutch Repair Café via its website, have since arisen in France, Germany, South Africa, the United States, and other countries. The original provides a central source for start-up tips and tools, as well as marketing advice to new Repair Cafés. As a result, the Repair Café has become a global network united by common ideals. Ironically, innovators are now looking back to old ways of doing things and applying them in today's cities in an effort to transform the way people relate to and think about the goods they consume.

★ 自我检测 2 删减答案

A Quick Fix in a Throwaway Culture

Planned obsolescence, <u>a practice whereby products are designed to have a limited period of usefulness（插入语）</u>, has been a cornerstone of manufacturing strategy for the past 80 years. This approach increases sales, but it also stands in stark contrast to a time <u>when goods were produced to be durable（定语从句）</u>. Planned obsolescence wastes materials as well as energy in making and shipping new products. It also reinforces the belief <u>that it is easier to replace goods than to mend them（同位语从句）</u>, <u>as repair shops are rare and repair methods are often specialized（原因状语从句）</u>. In 2009, an enterprising movement, <u>the Repair Café（插入语）</u>, challenged this widely accepted belief.

<u>More like a fair than an actual café（方式状语）</u>, the first Repair Café took place in Amsterdam, the Netherlands. It was the brainchild of former journalist Martine Postma, <u>who wanted to take a practical stand in a throwaway culture（定语从句）</u>. Her goals were straightforward: <u>reduce waste, maintain and perpetuate knowledge and skills, and strengthen community（同位语）</u>. Since the <u>inaugural Repair Café（时间状语）</u>, others have been hosted in theater foyers, community centers, hotels, and auditoriums. Participants bring all manner of damaged articles—<u>clothing, appliances,

furniture, and more（插入语）—to be repaired by a staff of volunteer specialists including tailors, electricians, and carpenters（后置定语）. While awaiting for service（时间状语从句）, patrons can enjoy coffee and snacks and mingle with their neighbors in need.

Though only about 3 percent of the Netherlands' municipal waste ends up in landfills（让步状语从句）, Repair Cafés still raise awareness about what may otherwise be mindless acts of waste by providing a venue for people to share and learn valuable skills that are in danger of being lost（方式状语）. It is easy to classify old but fixable items as "junk" in an era that places great emphasis on the next big thing（定语从句）. In helping people consider how the goods they use on a daily basis work and are made（状语）, Repair Cafés restore a sense of relationship between human beings and material goods.

Though the concept remained a local trend at first（让步状语从句）, international Repair Cafés, all affiliated with the Dutch Repair Café via its website（插入语）, have since arisen in France, Germany, South Africa, the United States, and other countries. The original provides a central source for start-up tips and tools, as well as marketing advice to new Repair Cafés. As a result, the Repair Café has become a global network united by common ideals（后置定语）. Ironically, innovators are now looking back to old ways of doing things and applying them in today's cities in an effort to transform the way people relate to and think about the goods they consume（目的状语）.

★ 自我检测 3

More than One Way to Dress a Cat

From Michelangelo's *David* to Vincent van Gogh's series of self-portraits to Grant Wood's iconic image of a farming couple in *American Gothi*, works by human artists have favored representations of members of their own species to those of other species. Indeed, when we think about animals depicted in well-known works of art, the image of dogs playing poker—popularized in a series of paintings by American artist C. M. Coolidge—may be the first and only one that comes to mind. Yet some of the earliest known works of art, including paintings and drawings tens of thousands of years old found on cave walls in Spain and France, portray animals. Nor has artistic homage to our fellow creatures entirely died out in the millennia since, as the example of one museum in Russia shows.

The State Hermitage Museum in St. Petersburg, one of Russia's greatest art museums, has long had a productive partnership with a much loved animal: the cat. For centuries, cats have guarded this famous museum, ridding it of mice, rats, and other rodents that could damage the art, not to mention scare off visitors. Peter the Great introduced the first cat to the Hermitage in the early eighteenth century. Continuing the tradition, Peter's daughter Elizaveta introduced the best and strongest cats in Russia to the Hermitage. Later Catherine the Great declared the cats to be official guardians of the galleries. Today, the museum holds a yearly festival honoring these faithful workers.

These cats are so cherished by the museum that officials recently commissioned original paintings to be made of six of them. In each, a cat is depicted upright in a humanlike pose and clothed in imperial-era Russian attire. The person chosen for this task, digital artist Eldar Zakirov, painted the cats in the style traditionally used by portrait artists, in so doing presenting the cats as noble individuals worthy of respect. One portrait, *The Hermitage Court Chamber Herald Cat*, includes an aristocratic tilt of feline ears as well as a stately sweep of tail emerging from the stiff scarlet and gold of royal court dress. The wise, thoughtful green eyes of the subject of *The Hermitage Court Outrunner Cat* mimic those of a trusted royal advisor. Some may find it peculiar to observe cats portrayed in formal court poses, but these felines, by protecting the museum's priceless artworks from destructive rodents, are benefactors of the museum as important as any human.

★ 自我检测 3 删减答案

More than One Way to Dress a Cat

From Michelangelo's *David* to Vincent van Gogh's series of self-portraits to Grant

Wood's iconic image of a farming couple in *American Gothi* (状语), works by human artists have favored representations of members of their own species to those of other species. Indeed, when we think about animals depicted in well-known works of art (时间状语从句), the image of dogs playing poker—popularized in a series of paintings by American artist C. M. Coolidge (插入语)—may be the first and only one that comes to mind. Yet some of the earliest known works of art, including paintings and drawings tens of thousands of years old found on cave walls in Spain and France (插入语), portray animals. Nor has artistic homage to our fellow creatures entirely died out in the millennia since, as the example of one museum in Russia shows (方式状语).

The State Hermitage Museum in St. Petersburg, one of Russia's greatest art museums (插入语), has long had a productive partnership with a much loved animal: the cat (同位语). For centuries, cats have guarded this famous museum, ridding it of mice, rats, and other rodents that could damage the art, not to mention scare off visitors (伴随状语). Peter the Great introduced the first cat to the Hermitage in the early eighteenth century. Continuing the tradition (伴随状语), Peter's daughter Elizaveta introduced the best and strongest cats in Russia to the Hermitage. Later Catherine the Great declared the cats to be official guardians of the galleries. Today, the museum holds a yearly festival honoring these faithful workers (后置定语).

These cats are so cherished by the museum that officials recently commissioned original paintings to be made of six of them (结果状语从句). In each, a cat is depicted upright in a humanlike pose and clothed in imperial-era Russian attire. The person chosen for this task, digital artist Eldar Zakirov (插入语), painted the cats in the style traditionally used by portrait artists, in so doing presenting the cats as noble individuals worthy of respect (目的状语). One portrait, *The Hermitage Court Chamber Herald Cat* (插入语), includes an aristocratic tilt of feline ears as well as a stately sweep of tail emerging from the stiff scarlet and gold of royal court dress (后置定语). The wise, thoughtful green eyes of the subject of *The Hermitage Court Outrunner Cat* mimic those of a trusted royal advisor. Some may find it peculiar to observe cats portrayed in formal court poses, but these felines, by protecting the museum's priceless artworks from destructive rodents(插入语), are benefactors of the museum as important as any human.

★ 自我检测 4

Transforming the American West Through Food and Hospitality

Just as travelers taking road trips today may need to take a break for food at a rest area along the highway, settlers traversing the American West by train in the mid-1800s often found themselves in need of refreshment. However, food available on rail lines was generally of terrible quality. To capitalize on the demand for good food, Fred Harvey, an English-born entrepreneur, decided to open his own restaurant business to serve rail customers. Beginning in the 1870s, he opened dozens of restaurants in rail stations and dining cars. These Harvey Houses, which constituted the first restaurant chain in the United States, were unique for their high standards of service and quality. The menu was modeled after those of fine restaurants, so the food was leagues beyond the abysmal fare travelers were accustomed to receiving in transit.

His restaurants were immediately successful, but Harvey was not content to follow conventional business practices. Although women did not traditionally work in restaurants in the nineteenth century, Harvey decided to try employing women as waitstaff. In 1883, he placed an advertisement seeking educated, well-mannered, articulate young women between the ages of 18 and 30. Response to the advertisement was overwhelming, and Harvey soon replaced the male servers at his restaurants with women. Those who were hired as "Harvey Girls" joined an elite group of workers, who were expected to complete a 30-day training program and follow a strict code of rules for conduct and curfews. In the workplace, the women donned identical black-and-white uniforms and carried out their duties with precision. Not only were such regulations meant to ensure the efficiency of the business and the safety of the workers, but they also helped to raise people's generally low opinion of the restaurant industry. In return for the servers' work, the position paid quite well for the time: $17.50 a month, plus tips, meals, room and board, laundry service, and travel expenses.

For as long as Harvey Houses served rail travelers through the mid-twentieth century, working there was a steady and lucrative position for women. Living independently and demonstrating an intense work ethic, the Harvey Girls became known as a transformative force in the American West, inspiring books, documentaries, and even a musical. Advancing the roles of women in the restaurant industry and the American workforce as a whole, the Harvey Girls raised the standards for restaurants and blazed a trail in the fast-changing landscape of the western territories.

★ 自我检测 4 删减答案

Transforming the American West Through Food and Hospitality

Just as travelers taking road trips today may need to take a break for food at a rest area along the highway（方式状语从句）, settlers traversing the American West by train in the mid-1800s（后置定语） often found themselves in need of refreshment. However, food available on rail lines was generally of terrible quality. To capitalize on the demand for good food（目的状语）, Fred Harvey, an English-born entrepreneur（插入语）, decided to open his own restaurant business to serve rail customers. Beginning in the 1870s（伴随状语）, he opened dozens of restaurants in rail stations and dining cars. These Harvey Houses, which constituted the first restaurant chain in the United States（插入语）, were unique for their high standards of service and quality. The menu was modeled after those of fine restaurants, so the food was leagues beyond the abysmal fare travelers were accustomed to receiving in transit（结果状语从句）.

His restaurants were immediately successful, but Harvey was not content to follow conventional business practices. Although women did not traditionally work in restaurants in the nineteenth century（让步状语从句）, Harvey decided to try employing women as waitstaff. In 1883, he placed an advertisement seeking educated, well-mannered, articulate young women between the ages of 18 and 30（后置定语）. Response to the advertisement was overwhelming, and Harvey soon replaced the male servers at his restaurants with women. Those who were hired as "Harvey Girls"（定语从句）joined an elite group of workers, who were expected to complete a 30-day training program and follow a strict code of rules for conduct and curfews（定语从句）. In the workplace（地点状语）, the women donned identical black-and-white uniforms and carried out their duties with precision. Not only were such regulations meant to ensure the efficiency of the business and the safety of the workers, but they also helped to raise people's generally low opinion of the restaurant industry. In return for the servers' work（状语）, the position paid quite well for the time: $17.50 a month, plus tips, meals, room and board, laundry service, and travel expenses（同位语）.

For as long as Harvey Houses served rail travelers through the mid-twentieth century（时间状语）, working there was a steady and lucrative position for women. Living independently and demonstrating an intense work ethic（伴随状语）, the Harvey Girls became known as a transformative force in the American West, inspiring books, documentaries, and even a musical（伴随状语）. Advancing the roles of women in the restaurant industry and the American workforce as a whole（伴随状语）, the Harvey Girls raised the standards for restaurants and blazed a trail in the fast-changing landscape of the western territories.

第三章

观点表达类题目

(*Expression of Ideas*)

技巧真经

一、文章发展题（Development）

A. 主旨题（Proposition）

题目要求添加或修改文章的主旨句或段落的主旨句，此题考查考生对文章主旨或段落主旨的概括能力。

★ 题目形式

More Than One Way to Dress a Cat

From Michelangelo's *David* to Vincent van Gogh's series of self-portraits to Grant Wood's iconic image of a farming couple in *American Gothic*, works by human artists have favored representations of members of their own species to those of other species. Indeed, when we think about animals depicted in well-known works of art, the image of dogs playing poker—popularized in a series of paintings by American artist C. M. Coolidge, may be the first and only one that comes to mind. Yet some of the earliest known works of art, including paintings and drawings tens of thousands of years old found on cave walls in Spain and France, portray animals. Nor has artistic homage to our fellow creatures entirely died out in the millennia since, **37** despite the many years that have passed between then and now.

Which choice most effectively concludes the paragraph by setting up the main focus of the passage?

A. NO CHANGE

B. with special attention being paid to domestic animals such as cats.

C. even though most paintings in museums are of people, not animals.

D. as the example of one museum in Russia shows.

⭐ 技巧真经

- 主旨题会考查考生对文章主旨和段落主旨的把握。文章主旨一般出现在第一段最后一句，段落主旨一般出现在段落第一句，题干中一般会出现 main focus、main topic、main claim 之类的字样，考生们可以根据此特征来判断题型。

- 当题目要求添加或修改文章主旨句时，考生需要把此题留到这篇文章的最后一题来做，先完成其余 10 道题。其余题目做完后，考生会对每一个分论点段的段意有基本了解，就可以通过概括分论点段的段意得出文章主旨句。

- 在添加或修改段落主旨句时，考生需要阅读并理解段落中的其余句子，通过段落的细节内容概括出本段主旨。

⭐ 例题

6 CWB also works with volunteers who are rigorously trained chemists. While some volunteers are concerned citizens who want to assist with public education campaigns, others hold actual chemistry training. The education background for water chemists is varied but includes many disciplines, including microbiology and geology. Students explore these related fields to develop a more comprehensive view of the variables that affect water quality.

Which choice provides the most effective introduction to the main topic of the paragraph?

A. NO CHANGE

B. Trained professionals provide invaluable resources to the water chemistry field.

C. CWB's work depends on the aid of volunteers in a variety of capacities.

D. Education background for water chemists involves studying sciences outside the chemistry field.

1. 答案

C。

2. 讲解

此题是段落主旨题，考生需要对段落中的其余句子进行阅读并理解，通过段落的细节内容概括出本段主旨。第二句意思是：虽然一些志愿者是一些担忧的公民，但还有一些是受过真正的化学训练的。第三句意思是：这些水质化学家的教育背景是非常多元的，包括微生物学和地质学。第四句意思是：学生们探索这些相关领域，发展了一种能影响水质因素的更全方位的角度。这些句子的意思概括起来就是志愿者的教育背景是非常多元的，所以选项C最符合，选项大意为：CWB的工作依赖有多种能力的志愿者的帮助。A选项的意思是CWB会与受过严格训练的化学家志愿者合作，这个选项太过片面，只符合第二句句意；B选项的意思是受过训练的专家给水质化学领域提供了非常有价值的资源，与A选项一样，只符合第二句句意；D选项的意思是水质化学家的教育背景涉及研究化学领域以外的科学，这个选项只符合第三句句意。

B. 论据题（Support）

题目要求添加或修改支持观点句的例子，此题考查观点和例子之间的总分关系。

★ 题目形式

Conceptualizing a game is only the beginning of a video game designer's job, however, no matter how good a concept is, it will never be translated into a video game unless it is communicated effectively to all the other members of the video game development team. A designer must generate extensive documentation and

38 <u>explain his or her ideas clearly</u> in order to ensure that the programmers, artists, and others on the team all share the same vision.

Which choice results in a sentence that best <u>supports</u> the point developed in this paragraph?

A. NO CHANGE

B. possess a vivid imagination

C. assess his or her motivations carefully

D. learn to accept constructive criticism

⭐ 技巧真经

- 论据题的题干中一般会出现 support 或 example 的字样，考生们可以根据这一特征来判断题型。

- 若题目要求添加或修改一个例子来支持段落的主旨句，即段首句，考生需要先阅读段落主旨句，了解其内容，再推测例子的内容。

- 若题目要求添加或修改一个例子来支持它的总说句，即例子所在句的前一句，考生则需要先阅读例子的前一句话，了解总说句内容，再推测例子的内容。

- 总分句之间的关系遵循两个原则：（1）总说句和分说句的句意方向一致；（2）分说句是总说句主语或宾语的具体化，即当我们看到总说句时，把总说句中的主语或宾语挑出来具体化，就可以预测出分说句了。例如，总说句是"Human activity can contribute to the environmental pollution."，句中主语是 human activity，宾语是

environmental pollution，那么就可以预测分说句的内容应该是什么样的人类活动会导致什么样的环境污染。

⭐ 例题

Conceptualizing a game is only the beginning of a video game designer's job, however, no matter how good a concept is, it will never be translated into a video game unless it is communicated effectively to all the other members of the video game development team. A designer must generate extensive documentation and <u>38 explain his or her ideas clearly</u> in order to ensure that the programmers, artists, and others on the team all share the same vision.

Which choice results in a sentence that best <u>supports</u> the point developed in this paragraph?

A. NO CHANGE

B. possess a vivid imagination

C. assess his or her motivations carefully

D. learn to accept constructive criticism

1. 答案

A。

2. 讲解

此题要求选择一句话支持它的总说句，所以我们需要看这句话的前一句，前一句的语意是"构思一个游戏只是一个电子游戏设计师工作的开始,无论这个构思有多好,它都无法转变成一个真正的电子游戏,除非它被有效地传达给电子游戏开发团队的其他成员"。例子所在句表达的意思是"一个设计师必须产出丰富的资料并且＿＿＿＿＿＿",and 后面并列的内容要与总说句对应。A 选项非常符合,"清晰地表达设计师的观点"与总说句中"将构思有效地传达给电子游戏开发团队的其他成员"呼应。B 选项是有生动的想象力,C 选项是仔细评估设计师的动机,D 选项是学会接受建设性的批评,这些都与总说句无关。

C. 焦点题(Focus)

题目要求基于句子与段落主旨的相关性,添加或删减句子。此题考查例子与主旨句及段落其他句子之间的统一性和相关性。

★ 题目形式

Fortunately, a new group of artists has discovered the murals, and efforts are underway to clean, restore, and repaint them. Once again, Siqueiros's "América Tropical" is leading the way. After a lengthy and complex restoration process, this powerful work is now a tourist attraction, complete with a visitor center and a rooftop viewing platform. **11** Advocates hope that Siqueiros's mural will once more serve as an inspiration, this time inspiring viewers to save and restore an important cultural and artistic legacy.

At this point, the writer is considering adding the following sentence.

When it was painted in 1932, Siqueiros's mural was considered offensive, but now it is acclaimed.

Should the writer make this addition here?

A. Yes, because it provides historical context for the changes discussed in the passage.

B. Yes, because it provides a useful reminder of how people once viewed Siqueiros's work.

C. No, because it unnecessarily repeats information from earlier in the passage.

D. No, because it makes a claim about Siqueiros's work that is not supported by the passage.

His restaurants were immediately successful, but Harvey was not content to follow conventional business practices. **17** Although women did not traditionally work in restaurants in the nineteenth century, Harvey decided to try employing women as waitstaff.

The writer is considering deleting the previous sentence. Should the writer make this change?

A. Yes, because it introduces information that is irrelevant at this point in the passage.

B. Yes, because it does not logically follow from the previous paragraph.

C. No, because it provides a logical introduction to the paragraph.

D. No, because it provides a specific example in support of arguments made elsewhere in the passage.

★ 技巧真经

- 焦点题的题干中会出现 addition 或 deleting 的字样，考生们可以根据这一特征来判定题型。

- 若题目询问是否应该添加此句，考生要考虑此句和段落主旨句的相关性，即此句是否能支持段落主旨。若支持，则添加；反之，则删掉。

- 若题目询问是否应该删减此句，我们要考虑此句与前后句的逻辑衔接。若无直接的逻辑衔接，则需删减；反之，则保留。

⭐ 例题

Although advocates of organic food maintain that organic produce is healthier than conventionally grown produce because it has more vitamins and minerals, this assertion is not supported by scientific research. For instance, one review published in *The American Journal of Clinical Nutrition* provided analysis of the results of comparative studies conducted over a span of 50 years; researchers consistently found no evidence that organic crops are more nutritious than conventionally grown ones in terms of their vitamin and mineral content. **18** Similarly, Stanford University researchers who examined almost 250 studies comparing the nutritional content of different kinds of organic foods with that of their nonorganic counterparts found very little difference between the two.

At this point, the writer is considering adding the following sentence.

The United States Department of Agriculture (USDA) reports that organic agricultural products are now available in approximately 20,000 markets specializing in natural foods.

Should the writer make this addition here?

A. Yes, because it adds a relevant research finding from a government agency.

B. Yes, because it supports the passage's argument that organic food is less nutritious than conventionally grown food.

C. No, because it is not relevant to the paragraph's discussion of scientific evidence.

D. No, because it introduces a term that has not been defined in the passage.

1. 答案

C。

2. 讲解

此题考查添加句子，我们要根据此句和段落主旨句的相关性来判断此句是否需要添加。段落主旨句为段落首句，意思为：尽管有机食品的支持者认为有机食品比传统产品更健康，因为它含有更多的维生素和矿物质，但是这个断言并没有科学研究的支持。从主旨句我们可以预测，段落的内容应该围绕"科学研究无法给予支持"的角度进行写作，而需要插入的句子的意思是"USDA的报告称有机农产品在将近20 000家专卖天然食品的超市出售"，这与主旨句无关，所以判断不应该添加，答案排除A、B选项；C、D选项可通过原因的正确与否来判断，C选项说这个句子与段落对于科学证据的讨论无关，完全正确；D选项说这个句子引出了一个在段落中没有定义过的术语，但该句并没有提到相关术语，所以错误。

His restaurants were immediately successful, but Harvey was not content to follow conventional business practices. 17 Although women did not traditionally work in restaurants in the nineteenth century, Harvey decided to try employing women as waitstaff. In 1883, he placed an advertisement seeking educated, well-mannered, articulate young women between the ages of 18 and 30. Response to the advertisement was overwhelming, and Harvey soon replaced the male servers at his restaurants with women. Those who were hired as "Harvey Girls" joined an elite group of workers, who were expected to complete a 30-day training program and follow a strict code of rules for conduct and curfews. In the workplace, the women donned identical black-and-white uniforms and carried out their duties with precision. Not only were such regulations meant to ensure the efficiency of the business and the safety of the workers, but also helped to raise people's generally low opinion of the restaurant industry.

第三章　观点表达类题目（Expression of Ideas）技巧真经

> The writer is considering deleting the previous sentence. Should the writer make this change?
>
> A. Yes, because it introduces information that is irrelevant at this point in the passage.
>
> B. Yes, because it does not logically follow from the previous paragraph.
>
> C. No, because it provides a logical introduction to the paragraph.
>
> D. No, because it provides a specific example in support of arguments made elsewhere in the passage.

1. 答案

C。

2. 讲解

此题考查删减句子。考生需要考虑删减的句子与前后句的关系，如果承接很紧密，就不能删减，反之，则可以删减。此题中要删减的句子是段落第一句，所以只要看它与下一句的关系是否紧密即可。第一个句子的意思是：Harvey 的餐馆非常成功，但是他不满足于跟随传统的商业模式。通过此句可以预测，下一句应该围绕如何不跟随传统商业模式的角度进行说明。第二句的意思是：尽管女性在 19 世纪没有在餐馆工作的传统，Harvey 还是决定尝试雇佣女性员工。该句非常具体地说明了 Harvey 如何不跟随传统模式，恰好紧密承接了上一句，不能删减，因此排除 A、B 选项。C、D 两个选项可通过判断原因是否正确进行选择，C 选项说的是这句话提供了很有逻辑的段落引出句，完全符合原文，正确；D 选项说的是它提供了一个具体的例子支持了文章的观点，但这一句并不是例子，而是总说句，所以错误。

D. 数据信息题（Quantitative information）

在新SAT文法考试的文章中会插入一些图表，目的是强化文章的精确性和有效性，涉及题目会要求选项符合图表信息，题目考查考生阅读比较简单的图表以及将数据信息与段落主旨相关联的能力。

★ 题目形式

Most of Greenland's interior is covered by a thick layer of ice and compressed snow known as the Greenland Ice Sheet. The size of the ice sheet fluctuates seasonally: in summer, average daily high temperatures in Greenland can rise to slightly above 50 degrees Fahrenheit, partially melting the ice; in the winter, the sheet thickens as additional snow falls, and average daily low temperatures can drop [12] to as low as 20 degrees.

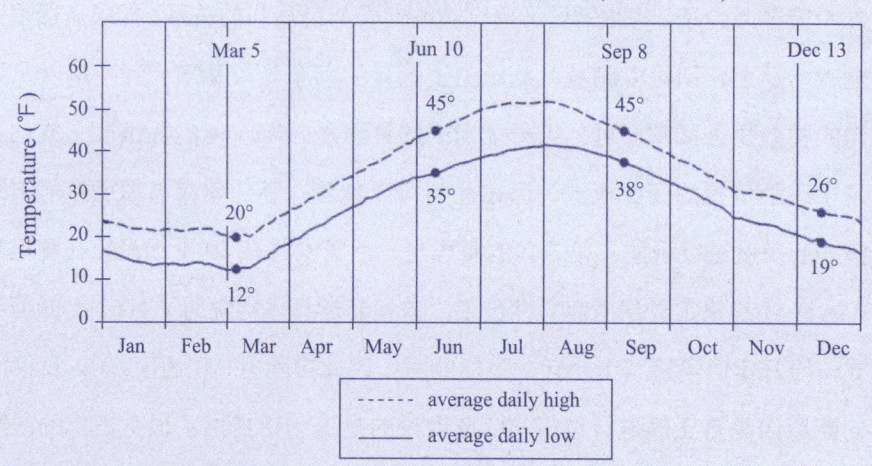

Average Daily High and Low Temperatures Recorded at Nuuk Weather Station, Greenland (1961—1990)

Mar 5: 20°, 12°
Jun 10: 45°, 35°
Sep 8: 45°, 38°
Dec 13: 26°, 19°

-------- average daily high
———— average daily low

Adapted from WMO. ©2014 by World Meteorological Organization.

Which choice most accurately and effectively represents the information in the graph?

A. NO CHANGE

B. to 12 degrees Fahrenheit.

C. to their lowest point on December 13.

D. to 10 degrees Fahrenheit and stay there for months.

★ 技巧真经

- 数据信息题中一定会出现图表，考生们可以根据这一特征来判断题型。

- 虽然说此题在题干中只是问哪个选项符合图表信息，但它绝不是仅仅考查考生读取图表信息的能力，在新 SAT 文法考试中，所有题目都是在文章段落的背景下提问，所以所有颗目都必须符合文章的写作要求。

- 数据信息可以作为证据支持前文观点，也可以作为证据反驳前文观点，所以做题时必须先阅读数据信息的前一句，由此句的语意预判数据信息的内容，再通过数据信息与图表信息的对应，选出正确选项。

★ 例题

It has long been known that the sea otters living along the West Coast of North America help keep kelp forests in their habitat healthy and vital. They do this by feeding on sea urchins and other herbivorous invertebrates that graze voraciously on kelp. With sea otters to keep the population of sea urchins in check, kelp forests can flourish. In fact, **24** two years or less of sea otters can completely eliminate sea urchins in a coastal area (see chart).

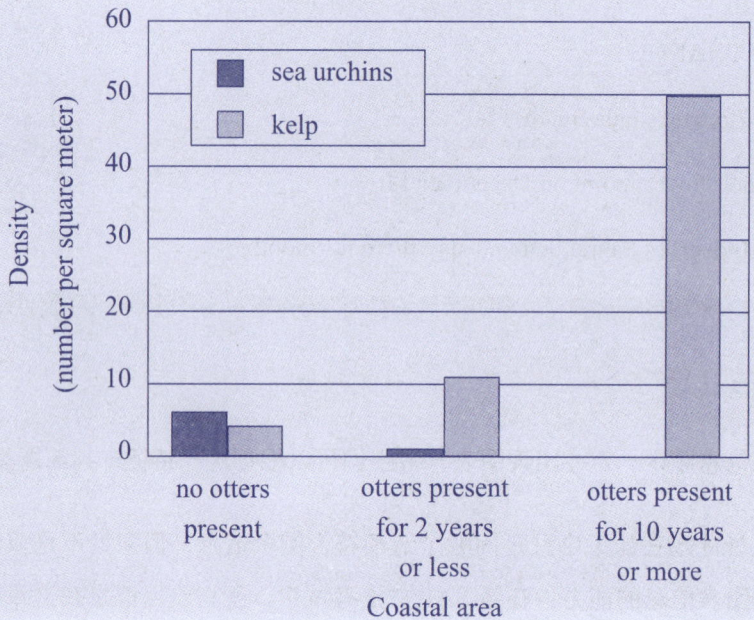

Effects of Sea Otter Presence on Kelp and Sea Urchin Density in Coastal Areas

[Bar chart showing Density (number per square meter) on y-axis (0 to 60) for three coastal area conditions:
- no otters present: sea urchins ~6, kelp ~4
- otters present for 2 years or less: sea urchins ~1, kelp ~11
- otters present for 10 years or more: sea urchins ~1, kelp ~50]

Adapted from David O. Duggins, "Kelp Beds and Sea Otters: An Experimental Approach." ©1980 by the Ecological Society of America.

Which choice offers an accurate interpretation of the data in the chart?

A. NO CHANGE

B. even two years or less of sea otter presence can reduce the sea urchin threat

C. kelp density increases proportionally as sea urchin density increases

D. even after sea otters were present for ten years or more, kelp density was still lower than sea urchin density

1. 答案

B。

2. 讲解

此题中引出数据信息的逻辑词是 in fact，说明该句是作为例子证明前一句观点句的，所以我们要先看观点句来得出本句的大体语意方向。观点句的意思是"因为海獭控制了海胆的数量，所以巨藻得以生长和繁荣"，数据信息应该与观点句的语意一致。我们再来看图，标题告诉我们此图展示了海獭的存在对海胆和巨藻密度的影响，其中分别显示出在没有海獭、海獭存在两年或更短时间和存在十年的情况下，海胆和巨藻的分布密度。下面我们来分析选项：A 选项说海獭存在两年或更短时间就可以完全清除海胆，与图不符，错误；B 选项说海獭存在两年或更短时间就可以减少海胆的威胁，既符合图表信息，又与观点句语意一致，正确；C 选项说巨藻密度的增加和海胆密度的增加是成比例的，这个选项既不符合图表信息，又不符合观点句语意，错误；D 选项说甚至在海獭存在了十年或更长时间之后，巨藻的密度仍然低于海胆的密度，这个选项既不符合图表信息，也不符合观点信息，所以错误。

二、文章结构题（Organization）

A. 逻辑顺序题（Logical sequence）

题目要求把句子放置在段落中最符合逻辑顺序的位置，考查句子之间的逻辑衔接。

⭐ 题目形式

[1] Perhaps the epitome of traditional methodology is the *Dictionary of American Regional English*, colloquially known as *DARE*. [2] Its fifth and final alphabetical volume—ending with "zydeco"—released in 2012, the dictionary represents decades of arduous work. [3] Over a six-year period from 1965 to 1970, university graduate students conducted interviews in more than a thousand communities across the nation. [4] Their goal was to determine what names people used for such everyday

objects and concepts as a submarine sandwich (a "hero" in New York City but a "dagwood" in many parts of Minnesota, Iowa, and Colorado) and a heavy rainstorm (variously a "gully washer," "pour-down," or "stump mover"). [5] The work that dictionary founder Frederic G. Cassidy had expected to be finished by 1976 was not, in fact, completed in his lifetime. [6] The wait did not dampen enthusiasm among scholars. Scholars consider the work a signal achievement in linguistics. **27**

To improve the cohesion and flow of this paragraph, the writer wants to add the following sentence.

Data gathering proved to be the quick part of the project.

The sentence would most logically be placed after

A. sentence 2.

B. sentence 3.

C. sentence 4.

D. sentence 5.

★ 技巧真经

- 首先判断句子的逻辑关系，常考逻辑有指代逻辑、转折逻辑、总分逻辑和主谓宾逻辑。接下来我会一一讲解不同逻辑的判定标准和预测技巧。

- 接着根据判定出的逻辑对句子的前一句或后一句进行预测，再回到段落中看哪一个句子与预测相符，最后进行选项对应。

1. 指代逻辑

判定标准："定冠词 + 名词"（the + *n.*）或"代词+名词"（this/these/that/those/his/her/its/their/such/another/other + *n.*）。

分析：当看到以"定冠词 + 名词"或"代词+名词"开始的句子时，我们会感觉到这个句子一定会与前面的句子形成承接关系，因为只有在前一句讲到一个事物、后一句话进行承接时才会出现这种情况。比如，我先说 "I like *Pride and Prejudice*."（我喜欢《傲慢与偏见》这本书），下一句想要继续说明这本书讲了什么，才会说 "This book is about..."，而this book在前一句是有所提及的。所以当看到包含指代逻辑的句子时，我们不需要把整个句子都看懂，而只要看代词后面或定冠词后面的名词部分，将其带到选项所在句的前文去对应，哪句话有这个名词部分，哪句话就是正确的。

技巧：直接看代词或定冠词后面的名词或名词词组，并将其与选项所在句的前一句对应，哪句话有对应的名词，就将选项放在这句话的后面。

2. 转折逻辑

判定标准：句子中有but、yet、however等转折词。

分析：当一句话由转折词引出，说明这句话与前一句话的关系一定是对比，所以前后句的意思应该相反，比如"梦想很丰满，但现实很骨感"中，丰满和骨感就是一对反义词；而这句话应该跟后一句话形成一个总分关系，因为转折词引出的经常是概括抽象的句子，下一句则要对它进行解释。

技巧：向两个方向进行预测。① 预测前一句，找寻句子的反义句（因为转折词连接的前后句意思相反）；② 预测后一句，找寻句子的分说句（根据分说句是总说句的主语或宾语的具体化原则）。

3. 总分逻辑

判定标准：如果判断这句话既不是指代逻辑，又不是转折逻辑，那我们就判定其为总分逻辑。

分析：判断为总分逻辑后，90%的情况会考查总说句，那么要向后预测分说句；

10%的情况会考查分说句，这时一定会有非常明显的举例提示词，如for example、some…some…等，这时要向前一句预测。

技巧：若判定是总说句，向后找分说句（总说句主宾的具体化）；若判定是分说句，向前找总说句（分说句主宾的概括化）。

4. 主谓宾逻辑

主谓宾逻辑的由来：如果我问大家，在"主语（S）+ 谓语（V）+ 宾语（O）"（简称S + V + O）这么一个简简单单的句子中存在任何逻辑吗？我估计很多考生会摇摇头说，这样一个句子哪有什么逻辑？又没有任何的逻辑词。很多人对英语句子逻辑的理解可能都停留在这种程度，认为一个句子有逻辑词就是有逻辑，而没有逻辑词就是没有逻辑，但是事实并不是这样。英语句子最有意思的地方就是，即便这个句子中没有任何逻辑词，它也和前后句有承接的逻辑关系。比方说，S + V + O这个句型中是没有逻辑词的，它的逻辑存在于主语的出现是为了承接上文内容，所以它是旧信息，而宾语的出现是为了引出下文，所以它是新信息，因此即便这个句子中没有任何逻辑词，我们也知道主语是跟前一句对应的，而宾语是跟后一句对应的。这个S + V + O的句子逻辑，还可以引申出其他句式的逻辑：如果一个句子用逗号隔开，我们可以推断其逗号之前的半句跟前一句承接，逗号之后的半句跟后一句承接；同样道理，一个句子如果用连词如and、if、because等进行连接，我们也可以推断连词之前的半句跟上一句承接，连词之后的半句跟下一句承接。

判定标准：主谓宾逻辑可以根据以下三种句型来进行判断。

① S + V + O（有主谓宾的完整句子）

② …, …（靠逗号隔开前后半句的句子）

③ …and/but/because/if…（靠连词隔开前后半句的句子）

技巧：① 在S + V + O结构的句子中，主语对应前一句，宾语对应后一句；

② 在逗号隔开的句子中，逗号之前的半句对应前一句，逗号之后的半句对应后一句；

③ 在and、but、because、if等连词隔开的句子中，连词之前的半句对应前一句，连词之后的半句对应后一句。

⭐ 例题

[1] A basic understanding of computer programming is essential. [2] In fact, many designers initially begin their pursuits as programmers. [3] Consider taking some general computer science courses as well as courses in artificial intelligence and graphics in order to increase your understanding of the technical challenges involved in developing a video game. [4] Courses in psychology and human behavior may help you develop important collaboration skills, while courses in the humanities, such as in literature and film, should give you the background necessary to develop effective narrative structures. [5] A designer also needs careful educational preparation. [6] Finally, because a designer should understand the business aspects of the video game industry, such as budgeting and marketing, you may want to consider taking some business courses. [7] Although demanding and deadline driven, video game design can be a lucrative and rewarding field for people who love gaming and have prepared themselves with the necessary skills and knowledge. 44

To make this paragraph most logical, sentence 5 should be

A. placed where it is now.

B. placed before sentence 1.

C. placed after sentence 3.

D. DELETED from the paragraph.

1. 答案

B。

2. 讲解

首先，我们需要判断 sentence 5 的逻辑：A designer also needs careful educational preparation. 此句中既没有指代逻辑词，也没有转折逻辑词，所以判断应该是总分逻辑。句子中有 also，表明此句是总说句，因此我们可以根据总分原则（分说句是总说句的主语或宾语的具体化）预测它后一句即分说句的语意应该是设计师需要什么样的教育准备。接下来，我们分析选项，A 选项是放在原位，后一句由 finally 一词引出，finally 表示一种并列逻辑，而且会引出总说句，和我们刚才对分说句的预判不符；B 选项是放在第一句前，第一句的意思是对电脑编程的基本理解非常重要，这符合我们的逻辑预判，因为电脑编程即是一种教育准备，该选项正确。C 选项是放在第三句后，第四句的意思是"心理学和人类行为学的课程可以帮助你发展重要的合作技能，而人文学科的课程，比如文学与电影，可以给你发展有效的记叙能力提供一些必要的背景"，看到这个句子时，很多考生可能会感觉此句和 sentence 5 也有一些关系，很难辨别，这时我们可以反向思考：此句是一个例子，这个例子的总说句应该是不同的课程可以培养不同的能力，这与 sentence 5 的语意不同，而且比 sentence 5 的语意更进一步，所以该选项错误。

B. 开篇句&结论句&过渡句题（Introductions, conclusions, and transitions）

题目要求添加或修改开篇句、结论句、过渡句或句子之间的逻辑连接词，考查考生对文章主题、段落关系和句子逻辑的判断能力。

第三章 观点表达类题目（Expression of Ideas）技巧真经

★ 题目形式

Studies have shown that employees are happier, healthier, and more productive when they work in an environment **27** <u>in which temperatures are carefully controlled.</u> New buildings may be designed with these studies in mind, but many older buildings were not, resulting in spaces that often depend primarily on artificial lighting. While employers may balk at the expense of reconfiguring such buildings to increase the amount of natural light, the investment has been shown to be well worth it in the long run—for both employees and employers.

Which choice provides the most appropriate <u>introduction</u> to the passage?

A. NO CHANGE

B. that affords them adequate amounts of natural light.

C. that is thoroughly sealed to prevent energy loss.

D. in which they feel comfortable asking managers for special accommodations.

As the map shows, "soda" is commonly heard in the middle and western portions of the United States; "pop" is frequently used in many southern states; and "coke" is predominant in the northeastern and southwest regions but used elsewhere as well. As interesting as Russ's findings are, though, their true value lies in their reminder that the Internet is not merely a sophisticated tool for collecting data but is also **33** <u>itself a rich source of data.</u>

Which choice most effectively <u>concludes</u> the sentence and paragraph?

A. NO CHANGE

B. where we can learn what terms people use to refer to soft drinks.

C. a useful way to stay connected to friends, family, and colleagues.

D. helpful to researchers.

9 Some vocational training programs were even created specifically for the benefit of returning veterans. One of the most unique examples in this category is the Culinary Institute of America, founded in 1946 to offer a novel curriculum for learning cooking stuff.

Which choice provides the most effective transition at this point?

A. NO CHANGE

B. Eventually, these numbers would taper off.

C. Nevertheless, the GI Bill had a long-lasting impact on the demographics of higher education.

D. Nor were these figures unique to one college.

He painted the mural's first two sections, featuring images of a tropical rainforest and a Maya pyramid, during the day. **2** Also, to avoid scrutiny, Siqueiros painted the final section of the mural, the centerpiece at night.

A. NO CHANGE

B. However,

C. Although,

D. Moreover,

⭐ 技巧真经

- 开篇句 & 结论句 & 过渡句题的题干中会出现 introduction、conclusion、transition 的字样或者带下划线的逻辑副词（如 moreover），考生们可以根据这些特征来判断题型。

- 若题目要求添加或修改开篇句，即文章首段第一句，因第一句和第二句是承接关系，我们只需看第二句，通过第二句话的语意判断开篇句即可。

- 若题目要求添加或修改结论句，会出现两种题干类型，一种题干会对结论句提出要求，遇到这种情况我们只需根据题干要求答题即可；另一种题干只是单纯地要求添加结论句，此时结论句要符合两个条件，第一要与前一句承接，第二要回扣文章主旨句，即文章首段末句，所以我们首先要看一下前一句语意，其次要看一下首段末句，即可得出结论句答案。

- 若题目要求添加或修改段落之间的过渡句，我们可以先观察一下四个选项的过渡句的句式结构，若句式呈现出 "..., ..." 的结构，即用逗号隔开前后半句，就要选择承上启下的过渡句，那么我们既要了解上一段的主旨，也要了解本段的主旨，上一段主旨我们通过看上一段段首句可知，本段主旨我们通过阅读本段其余句子，概括细节内容可知；若句式结构是简单的主谓宾结构，此题需要选择的过渡句只要引起下文即可，可以通过阅读下文细节内容概括得出。

- 若题目要求添加或修改句子之间的逻辑词，我们要根据前后两句的句意来判断。

★ 常考逻辑关系词总结

1. 并列逻辑

① 此外：also, additionally, in addition, moreover, furthermore, what is more, besides

② 除了：in addition to, apart from, aside from

2. 转折逻辑

① 但是：but, yet, while, whereas, however, nevertheless, nonetheless

② 虽然：despite, in spite of, notwithstanding

3. 举例逻辑

for example, for instance, such as, including, in fact

4. 结果逻辑

thus, therefore, thereby, hence, as a result, as a consequence, consequently, accordingly

5. 对比逻辑

by contrast, in contrast, in contrast to, on the contrary, conversely, instead（而是）= rather

6. 比较逻辑

uniformly（一致地）, likewise, similarly

7. 时间逻辑

firstly, initially（起初）, at first, next, then, subsequently（接下来）, finally, eventually, ultimately（最终）, at last

★ 例题

Studies have shown that employees are happier, healthier, and more productive when they work in an environment **1** in which temperatures are carefully controlled. New buildings may be designed with these studies in mind, but many older buildings were not, resulting in spaces that often depend primarily on artificial lighting. While employers may balk at the expense of reconfiguring such buildings to increase the amount of natural light, the investment has been shown to be well worth it in the long run—for both employees and employers.

Which choice provides the most appropriate introduction to the passage?

A. NO CHANGE

B. that affords them adequate amounts of natural light.

C. that is thoroughly sealed to prevent energy loss.

D. in which they feel comfortable asking managers for special accommodations.

1. 答案

C。

2. 讲解

此题要求选择一个开篇句，开篇句只要与第二句逻辑承接即可，所以我们要通过第二句的内容推导出开篇句的语意。第二句的意思是：新建筑的设计可能会考虑到这些研究，但很多古老的建筑都没有考虑这些，导致其空间往往主要依赖人造灯光照明。第二句中存在指代逻辑 these studies，说明前一句应该提及这些研究是什么，通过第二句内部的转折逻辑词 but，推断这些研究应该与 artificial lighting 相反。基于这些分析，我们来看选项：A 选项是说在这个环境里，温度是可控的，这与 lighting 无关，错误；B 选项说这个环境能提供充足的自然光，与 artificial lighting 形成对比，所以正确；C 选项说这个环境被完全密封以阻止能源消耗，与 lighting 无关，错误；D 选项说在这个环境里，员工会感觉很轻松地要求经理提供特殊的住处，与 lighting 无关，错误。

---

9 Some vocational training programs were even created specifically for the benefit of returning veterans. One of the most unique examples in this category is the Culinary Institute of America, founded in 1946 to offer a novel curriculum for learning cooking stuff.

Which choice provides the most effective transition at this point?

A. NO CHANGE

B. Eventually, these numbers would taper off.

C. Nevertheless, the GI Bill had a long-lasting impact on the demographics of higher education.

D. Nor were these figures unique to one college.

1. 答案

A。

2. 讲解

此题要求考生选出一个过渡句，我们先来观察一下四个选项的句式结构，发现都是主谓宾结构的句式，所以此过渡句只需要引起下文即可。接下来我们可以通过下文的细节内容推断出过渡句的语意。下文的大意是：这个类别中最独特的一个例子是美国烹饪学院，成立于1946年，为学习烹饪提供了一个全新的课程。通过此句我们可以预测过渡句应该会说到关于课程的内容。基于这些分析，我们来看选项：A选项说一些职业培训项目是特意为回来的老兵创立的，句中的职业培训项目与我们预测的课程内容相符，所以正确；B选项说这些数字会逐渐减少，与预测内容无关，错误；C选项说GI法案对高等教育的人口分布有一个长期的影响，与预测内容无关，错误；D选项说这些数据也不是一个大学独有的，与预测内容无关，错误。

Finally, researchers have found that 1-MCP actually increases susceptibility to some pathologies in certain apple varieties. For example, Empire apples are prone to a condition that causes the flesh of the apple to turn brown. Traditionally, apple producers have dealt with this problem by leaving the apples in the open air for three weeks before storing them in a controlled atmosphere with tightly regulated temperature, humidity, and carbon dioxide levels. As the graph shows, the flesh of untreated Empire apples that are first stored in the open air undergoes roughly five percent less browning than the flesh of untreated Empire apples that are immediately put into storage in a controlled environment. However, when Empire apples are treated with 1-MCP, their flesh turns brown when the apples are first stored in the open air, though not under other conditions. Although researchers continue to search for the right combination of factors that will keep fruits fresh and attractive, **33** the problem may be that consumers are overly concerned with superficial qualities rather than the actual freshness of the fruit.

33. The writer wants a conclusion that conveys how the shortcomings of 1-MCP presented in the passage affect the actions of people in the fruit industry. Which choice best accomplishes this goal?

A. NO CHANGE

B. many of the improvements to fruit quality they have discovered so far have required trade-offs in other properties of the fruit.

C. for now many fruit sellers must weigh the relative values of aroma, color, and freshness when deciding whether to use 1-MCP.

D. it must be acknowledged that 1-MCP, despite some inadequacies, has enabled the fruit industry to ship and store fruit in ways that were impossible before.

1. 答案

C。

2. 讲解

此题要求考生选择一个结论句，题干对结论句是有要求的，所以考生只要完成题干要求即可。题干说结论句要传达出 1-MCP 的缺点是如何影响水果行业人员行为的，所以正确选项必须要围绕这个内容进行说明。下面我们来分析选项：A 选项的意思是这个问题可能是消费者过度在意水果表面的质量，而不注重其实质上是否新鲜，此选项的中心点是消费者，与水果行业人员行为无关，错误；B 选项的意思是他们至今发现的对于水果质量的许多提升都需要用水果其他特性来交换，此选项中心点是水果质量，与题干无关，错误；C 选项的意思是现在许多水果的销售员在决定是否使用 1-MCP

时必须要衡量水果的气味、颜色和新鲜度的相对价值，此选项说到了水果行业人员的行为，与题干符合，正确；D 选项的意思是必须要承认的是，尽管 1-MCP 有一些不足，但它使得水果行业以过去不可能实现的方式运输和储存水果，也与水果行业人员无关，错误。

In 1932 the well-known Mexican muralist David Alfaro Siqueiros was commissioned to paint a mural on the second-story exterior wall of a historic building in downtown Los Angeles. Siqueiros was asked to celebrate tropical America in his work, he accordingly titled it "América Tropical." He painted the mural's first two sections, featuring images of a tropical rainforest and a Maya pyramid, during the day. **2** Also, to avoid scrutiny, Siqueiros painted the final section of the mural, the centerpiece at night.

A. NO CHANGE

B. However,

C. Although,

D. Moreover,

---

1. 答案

B。

2. 讲解

此题画线部分为逻辑副词，由此我们判断此题考查的是逻辑过渡词，需要通过前后两句的句意来判断两句话的逻辑关系。前一句的意思是"他在白天绘制了壁画的前两部分，前两部分以热带雨林和玛雅金字塔为特点"，后一句的意思是"为了避免检查，Siqueiros 在夜间画壁画的最后一部分"，两句话形成了白天和夜间的时间对比，所以应该选 B。

三、有效词句运用题（Effective Language Use）

A. 措辞题（Precision）

题目要求根据文章背景，选出最准确、最适合的词汇，此题考查考生词汇辨析和准确记忆能力。

★ 题目形式

Although advocates of organic food **16** preserve that organic produce is healthier than conventionally grown produce because it has more vitamins and minerals, this assertion is not supported by scientific research.

A. NO CHANGE

B. carry on

C. maintain

D. sustain

★ 技巧真经

- 此题需要考生先准确理解词汇所在句子的语意，通过语意判断所需词汇的含义，再通过对比选项，得出答案。

注：此题有助于考生们走出背单词的误区，那就是不能只背诵单词的词义，而一定要把单词带入句中，理解单词运用的场景。

★ 例题

A basic understanding of computer programming is essential. In fact, many designers initially begin their pursuits as programmers. Consider taking some general computer science courses as well as courses in artificial intelligence and graphics in order to increase your understanding of the technical challenges involved in developing a video game. Courses in psychology and human behavior may help you develop 42 emphatic collaboration skills, while courses in the humanities, such as in literature and film, should give you the background necessary to develop effective narrative structures.

A. NO CHANGE

B. paramount

C. eminent

D. important

1. 答案

D。

2. 讲解

对于措辞题，我们首先要理解词所在句子的语意，通过语意大体了解词汇的含义，本句语意是：心理学和人类行为学方面的课程可以帮助你提升 _____ 合作技能，而人文学科的课程，如文学和电影，会为你提升有效的记叙能力提供必要的背景。通过语意，我们可以看出要选择的形容词应该与 effective 方向一致，表达一种积极的语意。下面我们来分析选项：A 选项 emphatic 意为"强调的"，不太符合；B 选项 paramount 意为"重要的"，但它强调的是至关重要，比任何事情都重要，不太符合此句的意思；C 选项 eminent 的意思是"卓越的，非凡的"，一般用于形容能力非凡的专业人士，不符合此句的意思；D 选项 important 意为"重要的"，比较符合文章意思，正确。

B. 简洁性题（Concision）

此题要求表达简洁明了，不多余，不累赘。大道至简，语言表达亦是如此。

题目形式

When I left my office job as a website developer at a small company for a position that allowed me to work full-time from home, I thought I had it made: I gleefully traded in my suits and dress shoes for sweatpants and slippers, my frantic early-morning bagged lunch packing for a leisurely midday trip to my refrigerator. The novelty of this comfortable work-from-home life, however, **23** soon got worn off quickly. Within a month, I found myself feeling isolated despite having frequent email and instant messaging contact with my colleagues.

A. NO CHANGE

B. was promptly worn

C. promptly wore

D. wore

技巧真经

- 此题中一般会出现一个单词和一个词组意思相同，或两个单词表达同一词义的情况，考生只需要删减其中一个，即得出答案。

注：当题目中出现一个单词和一个词组意思相同时，要选择删减词组，因为单词要比词组更简洁，而简洁性原则是衡量语言表达好坏的根本性原则。所以在使用语言表达时，考生们要牢记一句话：**Keep it simple!**

简洁性原则：

(1) 单词 > 词组 > 句子；

(2) 在修饰名词时，形容词 > 非谓语动词 > 定语从句；

(3) 主动语态 > 被动语态；

(4) 动词 > 名词。

记住上述四大简洁性原则，说不定你的写作分数就会更高哦！

★ 例题

> Artificial light sources are also costly aside from lowering worker productivity. They typically constitute anywhere from 25 to 50 percent of a building's energy use. When a plant in Seattle, Washington, was redesigned for more natural light, the company was able to enjoy annual electricity cost reductions of $500,000 8 each year.
>
> A. NO CHANGE
>
> B. every year.
>
> C. per year.
>
> D. DELETE the underlined portion and end the sentence with a period.

1. 答案

D。

2. 讲解

在此题中，我们发现句子里的 annual（每年）和 each year 同义，说明出现了重复现象，因此要把 each year 删掉，句子才能则简洁明了，所以选择 D。

C. 风格&语气题（Style and tone）

此题要求考生选择的词汇必须符合文章规范性写作的风格，考查书面语与口头表达的区别。

第三章 观点表达类题目（Expression of Ideas）技巧真经

⭐ 题目形式

The menu was modeled after those of fine restaurants, so the food was leagues beyond the 16 sinister fare travelers were accustomed to receiving in transit.

Which choice best maintains the tone established in the passage?

A. NO CHANGE

B. surly

C. abysmal

D. icky

⭐ 技巧真经

- 风格 & 语气题的题干中通常会出现 tone 或 style 或 pattern 这些字样，考生们可以根据此特征来判定题型。

- 选择的词语必须是正式的书面语，并且要符合段落的语意方向。

- 选择的句子必须与原文的句式结构形式一致。

⭐ 例题

The plainer rooms are more sparsely furnished. Their architectural features, furnishings, and decorations are just as true to the periods they represent. One of my favorite rooms in the whole exhibit, in fact, is an 1885 summer kitchen. The room is simple but spacious, with a small sink and counter along one wall, a cast-iron wood stove and some hanging pots and pans against another wall, and 19 a small table under a window of the third wall. Aside from a few simple wooden chairs placed near the edges of the room, the floor is open and obviously well worn.

> 19. Which choice most closely matches the stylistic pattern established earlier in the sentence?
>
> A. NO CHANGE
>
> B. a small table is under the third wall's window.
>
> C. the third wall has a window and small table.
>
> D. the third wall has a small table against it and a window.

1. 答案

A。

2. 讲解

此题题干中出现了 pattern 一词，所以我们判定是风格 & 语气题，此题要求选择一个符合该句风格和形式的选项，即我们要分析这句话中其他成分的结构形式，然后推断出画线部分的形式。画线部分所在句是一个并列结构的句式，画线部分是并列的一部分，所以只要判断其他并列成分的形式，画线部分形式即可知。下面我们来分析一下这个句子，其主句是 "The room is simple but spacious"，后面的并列内容都为独立主格结构，独立主格结构的构成公式为 "with sb./sth. + 介词短语 / 分词 / 形容词 / 名词 / 不定式"，由此我们可以看出本句中并列的内容都是 "with sth. + 介词短语" 的结构，所以 A 选项符合要求，而 B、C、D 三个选项都是完整的句子，因此错误。

D. 句法题（Syntax）

此题要求把单独的两个句子有效地结合起来，以提升句子的逻辑性和流畅性。

★ 题目形式

9 <u>The result was an explosion of mural painting that spread throughout California and the southwestern United States in the 1970s. It was the Chicano mural movement.</u> Hundreds of large, colorful new murals depicting elements of Mexican American life and history appeared during this period, some in designated cultural locations but many more in abandoned lots, on unused buildings, or painted on infrastructure such as highways and bridges. Many of these murals can still be seen today, although some have not been well maintained.

Which choice most effectively <u>combines</u> the underlined sentences?

A. The result was an explosion, the Chicano mural movement, of mural painting that spread throughout California and the southwestern United States in the 1970s.

B. The result was the Chicano mural movement, an explosion of mural painting that spread throughout California and the southwestern United States in the 1970s.

C. The explosion of mural painting that spread throughout California and the southwestern United States in the 1970s was the resulting Chicano mural movement.

D. An explosion of mural painting resulted and it spread throughout California and the southwestern United States in the 1970s; it was the Chicano mural movement.

★ 技巧真经

- 句法题的题干中会出现 combines 之类的字样，考生们可以根据此特征来判定题型。

- 首先，合并的句子要符合原句之间的逻辑，所以先要阅读两个独立的句子，通过句意判断两句之间的逻辑，用正确的逻辑词连接两句话。

- 其次，合并的句子要符合简洁性原则，通过简洁性原则排除不符合的选项。（请参照前文中简洁性原则的讲解进行排除。）

⭐ 例题

But perhaps even more importantly, librarians function as first responders for their communities' computer needs. Since one of the fastest growing library services is public access computer use, there is great demand for computer instruction. 7 <u>In fact, librarians' training now includes courses on research and Internet search methods. Many of whom teach classes in Internet navigation, database and software use, and digital information literacy.</u> While these classes are particularly helpful to young students developing basic research skills, but adult patrons can also benefit from librarian assistance in that they can acquire job-relevant computer skills. Free to all who utilize their services, public libraries and librarians are especially valuable, because they offer free resources that may be difficult to find elsewhere, such as help with online job.

Which choice most effectively combines the underlined sentences?

A. In fact, librarians' training now includes courses on research and Internet search methods; many librarians teach classes in Internet navigation, database and software use, and digital information literacy is taught by them.

B. In fact, many librarians, whose training now includes courses on research and Internet search methods, teach classes in Internet navigation, database and software use, and digital information literacy.

C. Training now includes courses on research and Internet search methods; many librarians, in fact, are teaching classes in Internet navigation, database and software use, and digital information literacy.

D. Including courses on research and Internet search methods in their training is, in fact, why many librarians teach classes in Internet navigation, database and software use, and digital information literacy.

1. 答案

B。

2. 讲解

此题题干中有 combines 的字样，所以判定这是句法题。合并句子第一要符合句意逻辑，第二要简洁，所以我们先来分析划线的两个句子。从两句话的句意逻辑来看，两句话应该属于并列逻辑，因为一句话是在讲图书管理员的培训，另一句话是在讲图书管理员教授的课程。我们发现两个句子的主题都是图书管理员，所以可以合并成主语是 librarians 的一句话，主语发出两个动作，把两个句子有效地结合在一起，B 选项非常符合这个条件；A、C 两个选项虽然符合逻辑，但是不如 B 选项简洁，一个句子一定比两个并列的句子要简洁；D 选项语意出现了错误，直接排除。

第四章

标准语法类题目
(*Standard English Conventions*) 技巧真经

一、句子结构题（Sentence Structure）

A. 句子边界题（Sentence boundaries）

题目要求识别或修正不完整句子、句子片段和连排句（run-on），考查考生对句子结构的划分及判定能力。

★ 题目形式

> Thus, businesses can install light tubes, **10** <u>these are</u> pipes placed in workplace roofs to capture and funnel sunlight down into a building's interior. Glass walls and dividers can also be used to replace solid walls as a means through distributing natural light more freely. Considering the enormous costs of artificial lighting, both in terms of money and productivity, investment in such improvements should be a natural choice for businesses.
>
> A. NO CHANGE
>
> B. they are
>
> C. which are
>
> D. those being

★ 技巧真经

- 若考生们分析句子成分时发现句子缺少谓语或者句子是连排句，则可判定该题是句子边界题。

- 我们要明确完整句子的标准结构有主谓宾、主系表和主谓三种，即句子中必须有谓语动词或系动词，若把句子中的谓语变成动词的分词（*v.*-ed/*v.*-ing）或不定式（to + *v.*）形式，一定会出现缺少谓语的问题。

注：在一个简单句中把谓语变成动词的分词或不定式形式，考生们会很容易识别

第四章　标准语法类题目（Standard English Conventions）技巧真经

出问题，但如果句子的主语后加了许多修饰语，使主语和谓语离得相对比较远，这时谓语再变成动词的分词或不定式形式，即 S + 修饰语 + *v.*-ed/*v.*-ing/to *v.* + O，很多考生可能就识别不出来，所以考生们要注意这种情况。

- 我们要明确三种错误的句子连接方式，即连排句 (run-on)，分别是逗号连接两个句子 (S1 + V1 + O1, S2 + V2 + O2)、副词连接两个句子 (S1 + V1 + O1, *adv.* + S2 + V2 + O2)、两个连词连接两个句子 (连词 + S1 + V1 + O1, 连词 + S2 + V2 + O2)，如 Although + S1 + V1 + O1, but + S2 + V2 + O2。

注：在这三种连排句中，副词连接两个句子的迷惑性是最强的，原因是很多考生会把副词误认为连词，并因此忽略问题。接下来，我会把高频考查的逻辑副词总结出来，大家背诵下来就没有问题了。

转折副词：**nonetheless, nevertheless, however**

结果副词：**therefore, thereby, consequently, hence, thus, as a result, as a consequence, accordingly**

并列副词：**also, moreover, furthermore, in addition, besides, what is more, additionally**

时间副词：**firstly, initially, at first, then, subsequently, finally, eventually, ultimately, at last**

★ 例题

Viewing the exhibit, I was amazed by the intricate details of some of the more ornately decorated rooms. I marveled at a replica of a salon (a formal living room) dating back to the reign of French king Louis XV. Built into the dark paneled walls are bookshelves stocked with leather-bound volumes. The couch and chairs, in keeping with the style of the time, are characterized by elegantly curved arms and

16 legs, they are covered in luxurious velvet. A dime-sized portrait of a French aristocratic woman hangs in a golden frame.

A. NO CHANGE

B. legs, the couch and chairs

C. legs and

D. legs,

1. 答案

C。

2. 精讲

在此题中，画线部分所在句呈现了连排句比较简单的一种形式 "S1 + V1 + O1，S2 + V2 + O2"，第一个主句是 "The couch and chairs are characterized by elegantly curved arms and legs"，第二个主句是 "they are covered in luxurious velvet"，所以我们需要把第二个句子修改成不完整的句子，they 指代的是 the couch and chairs，说明第二句和第一句共用一个主语，所以我们可以把第二句的主语省略，用 and 连接即可，所以 C 选项正确。A、B、C 三个选项都是连排句形式，错误。

B. 从属连词和并列连词题（Subordination and coordination）

题目要求识别句子内部连接的从属连词和并列连词的逻辑关系。

第四章　标准语法类题目（Standard English Conventions）技巧真经

★ 题目形式

She maintains an objective tone for most of the book, **9** and the final chapter of *Translated Woman* offers a personal reflection on Behar's struggle to define her own cultural identity.

A. NO CHANGE

B. when

C. if

D. but

★ 技巧真经

- 选项中会出现从属连词（如 if、when、although）或并列连词（如 but、and），考生可据此判断题型。

- 此类题目通过句意判断逻辑即可选出正确答案。

★ 例题

She maintains an objective tone for most of the book, **9** and the final chapter of *Translated Woman* offers a personal reflection on Behar's struggle to define her own cultural identity.

A. NO CHANGE

B. when

C. if

D. but

1. 答案

D。

2. 精讲

此题选项中出现了并列连词 but 和 and 及附属连词 when 和 if，所以判断此题是从属连词和并列连词题。我们要通过理解句意判断前后句的逻辑：画线部分前一句出现了 objective 一词，说的是"她的大部分书是以客观的语气进行写作的"；后一句出现了 personal 一词，说的是"*Translated Woman* 一书的最后一章对 Behar 界定自身文化身份的斗争提供了个人的反思"。前后句呈现出对比关系，需要用对比逻辑词，因此答案是 D 选项。

C. 平行结构题（Parallel structure）

题目要求识别句子并列结构中出现的不平行问题，考查考生对平行结构的理解。

★ 题目形式

> Hundreds of large, colorful new murals depicting elements of Mexican American life and history appeared during this period, some in designated cultural locations but many more in abandoned lots, on unused buildings, or **9** painted on infrastructure such as highways and bridges.
>
> A. NO CHANGE
>
> B. They were painted on
>
> C. On
>
> D. DELETE the underlined portion.

★ 技巧真经

● 英语中的并列结构即平行结构，就像中文里的排比结构一样，具有形式上的美感。

- 首先，要懂得识别平行结构标志词，只要划线句中存在平行结构标志词，即可判断此题考查平行结构。

  平行结构标志词 { 连词：and, or, but, yet, while, whereas

  短语：not only…but also…, both…and…, either…or…, neither…nor…, between…and…, from…to…, not…but…, …rather than…

- 其次，知道如何判断平行方式，高频考查的平行方式有单词平行、谓语动词平行和词组平行三种方式，可以根据不同的平行方式进行选择。

① 单词平行，即相同词性的单词并列，如 "*n.* and *n.*"，这种平行方式比较简单，只要保证前后词性一致即可。

② 谓语动词平行，要注意一种句式结构，S + V1 + O1 and V2 + O2，这种结构中并列的两个句子因为主语一致，所以第二句话的主语会省略，这时前后的谓语动词平行，这两个动词必须在时态和人称上保持一致。

③ 词组平行包含动词不定式、现在分词和介词短语的平行：

a. to do and to do/to do and do

   to do, do and do/to do, to do and to do

注：动词不定式平行时，有两种方式，**to** 可以省略也可以不省略，若不省略，那么所有并列的不定式就都不要省略 **to**；若省略，一定要从第二个并列的不定式开始省略。

b. doing, doing and doing

c. at A and B

   at A…and at B

注：介词短语平行时，难点在于介词的省略，比如 **at A** 和 **at B** 并列，若 A 后面没

有任何修饰成分，则第二个介词短语中的介词可以省略；若 A 后面还有其他的修饰成分，为避免歧义，则第二个介词短语中的介词需要保留。

★ 例题

Studies have shown that employees are happier, **1** healthier, and more productive when they work in an environment **2** in which temperatures are carefully controlled. New buildings may be designed with these studies in mind, but many older buildings were not, resulting in spaces that often depend primarily on artificial lighting. While employers may balk at the expense of reconfiguring such buildings to increase the amount of natural light, the investment has been shown to be well worth it in the long run—for both employees and employers.

A. NO CHANGE

B. healthy, and more

C. healthier, and they are

D. healthier, being more

1. 答案

A。

2. 精讲

看到画线部分有 and，知道这是平行结构标志词，所以判定此题考查平行结构。接下来我们要判断这道题考查的平行方式，通过阅读画线句可知，此句中平行的成分是三个形容词的比较级，所以 A 选项正确；B 选项 healthy 不是比较级，错误；C 选项 and 后是一个句子，不符合平行结构要求，错误；D 选项 being more 中的 being 是累赘表达，不简洁，所以错误。

D. 悬垂修饰语题（Modifier placement）

题目要求识别和修改修饰语放置错误的问题，考查考生对于悬垂修饰语的判断能力。

☆ 题目形式

> Within a month, I found myself feeling isolated despite having frequent email and instant messaging contact with my colleagues. Having become frustrated trying to solve difficult problems, **24** no colleagues were nearby to share ideas.
>
> A. NO CHANGE
>
> B. colleagues were important for sharing ideas.
>
> C. ideas couldn't be shared with colleagues.
>
> D. I missed having colleagues nearby to consult.

☆ 技巧真经

对于此类题型，有一些高频的句式结构会出现悬垂修饰语问题，只要考生背下这些句式结构，在考试时能识别出它们，即可得出答案。同时，考生也可以通过这些句式来判断题型。

1. *v.*-ing/*v.*-ed/*adj.* ＋ S ＋ V ＋ O

在由现在分词、过去分词或形容词引导的伴随状语的句型结构中，主句的主语和伴随状语的主语必须一致，若发现主句的主语无法发出伴随状语的动作或者不能成为动作的接受者，则该句需要修改。

2. (in order) to do…, S ＋ V ＋ O

在有目的状语的句型结构中，in order 可以省略，主句的主语和目的状语的主语一致，若发现主句的主语无法发出目的状语的动作，则该句需要修改。

3. before/after doing…, S+V+O

在有 before 或 after 引导的时间状语的句型结构中，主句的主语和时间状语的主语一致，若发现主句的主语无法发出时间状语的动作，则该句需要修改。

4. when/although/while/if (S+V)+v.-ed/v.-ing/prep.+n./adj./n., S+V+O

在有状语从句的句型结构中，若省略主谓结构，说明主句的主语和状语从句的主语一致，若主句的主语无法发出状语从句的动作或成为动作的接受者，则该句需要修改。例如：Although a boy, Tom likes flowers. 句中 although 引导的让步状语从句中省略了 he is，Tom 是该从句的主语。

5. by/through doing…, S+V+O

在有 by 或 through 引导的方式状语的句型结构中，主句的主语和方式状语的主语一致，若主句的主语无法发出方式状语的动作，则该句需要修改。

6. N, S+V+O

在有同位语的句式结构中，同位语 N 解释主语 S，表明同位语和主语应该是同一类别，若同位语和主句的主语类别不同，则该句需要修改。例如：A student, Tom likes swimming. 句中同位语 a student 解释主句的主语 Tom，两者是同一类别。

7. in addition to/besides/apart from/aside from+doing sth., S+V+O

当上述递进词后跟着 v.-ing 结构时，我们要想到悬垂修饰语问题，若主句的主语无法发出 v.-ing 的动作，则该句需要修改。例如：In addition to reading books, students should always watch movies. 句中主句的主语 students 也是 reading books 的动作发出者。

8. prep.+n., S+V+O

在有介词结构的句式结构中，主句的主语和介词结构的主语一致，若主句的主语无法发出介词结构的动作，则该句需要修改。

⭐ 例题

As I walked through the exhibit, I overheard a visitor's remark, "You know, that grandfather clock actually runs. Its glass door swings open, and the clock can be wound up." **21** <u>Dotted with pin-sized knobs, another visitor noticed my fascination with a tiny writing desk and its drawers.</u> "All of those little drawers pull out. And you see that hutch? Can you believe it has a secret compartment?" Given the exquisite craftsmanship and level of detail I'd already seen, I certainly could.

A. NO CHANGE

B. Another visitor, dotted with pin-sized knobs, noticed my fascination with a tiny writing desk and its drawers.

C. Another visitor dotted with pin-sized knobs noticed my fascination with a tiny writing desk and its drawers.

D. Another visitor noticed my fascination with a tiny writing desk and its drawers, dotted with pin-sized knobs.

1. 答案

D。

2. 精讲

阅读画线句时我们发现这是一个有伴随状语的句型"v.-ed…, S + V + O",看到此句型我们就要想到悬垂修饰语问题,也就是要确认伴随状语的主语是否与主句的主语一致。主句的主语是 another visitor,伴随状语的意思是"点缀着胸针大小的球型把手",很明显 visitor 不能发出伴随状语的动作或成为该动作的接受者,所以 A 选项排除;B 选项 dotted with pin-sized knobs 作为插入语修饰 visitor,也是错误的;C 选项 dotted with pin-sized knob 作为 visitor 的后置定语修饰 visitor,是错误的;D 选项中的 dotted with pin-sized knob 放在 drawers（抽屉）后面，修饰抽屉，语意正确。

E. 时态题（Shifts in verb tense, mode, and voice）

该题型考查考生对各个时态的辨析及对时态转换不恰当的识别和修改。

★ 题目形式

> According to Box, a leading Greenland expert, tundra fires in 2012 from as far away as North America produced great amounts of soot, some of it drifted over Greenland in giant plumes of smoke and then 18 <u>fell</u> as particles onto the ice sheet.
>
> A. NO CHANGE
>
> B. falls
>
> C. will fall
>
> D. had fallen

★ 技巧真经

- 时态题题目会在谓语部分画线，选项中会出现各种时态的变化，考生可以据此特征来判断题型。

- 若画线部分所在句中没有可以明确表示本句时态的时间标志词，错误通常是过去时态和现在时态的混用，考生需要通过语意判断时态。比如，在描述客观事实或文学作品内容时，应该用一般现在时，若句中出现过去时态，则需要修改。

- 若画线部分所在句中有时间标志词，我们可以通过时间标志词确定句子时态，发现时态不符合，则需要修改。

★ SAT 文法高频考查时态辨析

1. 一般现在时

主要表示经常、反复发生的动作或行为及现在的某种情况。

2. 现在进行时

主要表示现阶段或说话时正在进行的动作及行为。

3. 一般过去时

主要表示过去发生的动作或存在的状态，也可以表示过去习惯性、经常性的动作。常考的时间标志词有 from 1999 to/until 2001、in 2010、last month 等。

4. 现在完成时

主要表示过去发生或已经完成的动作对现在造成的影响或结果，或者过去已经开始、持续到现在的动作或状态。常考的时间标志词有 since、in the past few years 等。

5. 过去完成时

主要表示在过去某动作之前完成的行为，即大背景为过去的时间，发生了两个动作，发生在先的动作用过去完成时，发生在后的动作用一般过去时，例如：Yesterday, Tom found that the menu of the restaurant had been changed.

6. 一般将来时

主要表示将要发生的动作及打算、计划或准备做的事情。常考的时间标志词有 next Friday、tomorrow、in a few days 等。

⭐ 例题

Not all research into regional English varieties **28** requires such time, effort, and resources, however. Today's researchers have found that the veritable army of trained volunteers traveling the country conducting face-to-face interviews can sometimes be replaced by another army: the vast array of individuals volunteering details about their lives—and, inadvertently, their language—through social media. Brice Russ of Ohio State University, for example, has employed software to sort through postings on one social media cite in search of particular words and phrases of interest as well as the location from which users are posting. From these data, he was able, among other things, to confirm regional variations in people's terms for soft drinks.

A. NO CHANGE

B. are requiring

C. have required

D. required

1. 答案

A。

2. 精讲

此题画线部分是动词，四个选项都是该动词不同的时态变化，所以判定此题是时态题。此句中没有时间标志词，所以我们要想到问题可能在于现在时态和过去时态的混用。我们发现段落中其他句子都是现在时态，说明此句也应该是现在时态，所以排除 D 选项；此句意思是"不是所有关于地区英语多样性的研究都需要这么多的时间、精力和资源",表述了一个客观事实,所以用一般现在时即可,答案选择 A。

F. 人称混淆题（Shifts in pronoun person and number）

该题型考查考生对人称的辨析及对人称转换不恰当的识别和修改。

★ 题目形式

> Because today's students can expect to hold multiple jobs—some of which may not even exist yet—during **44** our lifetime, studying philosophy allows them to be flexible and adaptable.
>
> A. NO CHANGE
>
> B. one's
>
> C. his or her
>
> D. their

★ 技巧真经

- 人称混淆题题目会在代词部分画线,选项中会出现各种不同的人称代词或物主代词,考生可以据此特征来判断题型。

- 做题时要清楚第一人称、第二人称、第三人称所有人称代词和物主代词的形式,通过语意判断句中需要使用哪种人称,再进行选择。

人称辨析

人称代词		第一人称	第二人称	第三人称
主格	单数	I	you	he, she, it
	复数	we	you	they

宾格	单数	me	you	him, her, it
	复数	us	you	them

物主代词		第一人称	第二人称	第三人称
形容词性	单数	my	your	his, her, its
	复数	our	your	their
名词性	单数	mine	yours	his, hers, its
	复数	ours	yours	theirs

⭐ 例题

Because today's students can expect to hold multiple jobs—some of which may not even exist yet—during 44 our lifetime, studying philosophy allows them to be flexible and adaptable.

A. NO CHANGE

B. one's

C. his or her

D. their

1. 答案

D。

2. 精讲

此题画线部分是代词，四个选项都是不同的人称，由此我们可以判定此题是人称混淆题。接下来我们需要通过代词所在句的语义判定代词到底指代什么，才能确定选择哪一个人称代词。本句句意是：因为今天的学生将来可能会有很多的工作——其中一些工作可能现在还不存在——在_____的生命中，学习哲学会让他们更灵活且适应性强。通过语意我们得知代词指代的是 students，所以应该是第三人称，代词要与其指代的名词单复数一致，所以选择 D；A 选项 our 是第一人称，所以错误；B、C 选项是单数代词，所以错误。

二、标准用法题（Conventions of Usage）

A. 指代题（Pronoun clarity）

题目要求识别并修改模糊不清的代词问题，即一个代词有多个名词可以指代或没有任何名词可以指代。该题型考查考生对指代不明或空指的判断能力。

★ 题目形式

Even more rigorous are the hurdles that pastry chefs must surmount to achieve CMPC status. Only eleven people in the United States currently hold this title. In order to be considered, **9** they must endure an eight-day-long practical exam that showcases their culinary skills; the prize affords membership in an elite cadre of pastry professionals and bestows valuable name recognition and clout in the culinary world.

A. NO CHANGE

B. he or she

C. candidates

D. those

★ 技巧真经

● 指代题题目会在代词部分画线，句中会出现指代不明或是空指问题，考生可以据此特征来判断题型。

- 指代不明即句中只有一个代词，却有多个名词可以指代，比如题目画线部分是 they，句中却有两个复数名词可以指代。修改方法是通过语意判断出代词指代哪一个名词，在答案中指代清楚即可。

- 空指即句中出现了代词，却没有名词可以指代。考生们要牢记，在 SAT 文法考试中所有代词只能指代名词，尤其要注意 it、this、that、which 这四个代词，在托福或雅思考试中经常可以看到它们指代句子或指代一件事的情况，但在 SAT 严谨的语法要求中，它们只能指代名词。

★ 例题

> Bats play a vital role in ecosystems, providing billions of dollars worth of insect-suppression and pollination services to farmers around the United States. But now, bats face a serious threat: white-nose syndrome (WNS), a fungal disease that causes a loss of body fat, unusual winter behavior, and even death. Since the first documentation of the disease in 2006, between 5.7 and 6.7 million North American bats have perished from a disease referred to as WNS, with some bat habitats experiencing population declines of more than 90 percent. As of 2014, twenty-five states and five Canadian provinces have confirmed cases of WNS; the affected region now reaches as far west as the Missouri-Kansas border.
>
> Scientists have determined that the cause of white-nose syndrome is a fungus—Pseudogymnoascus destructans—that flourishes in cold, wet environments and reproduces by generating spores that can lodge in the floors and walls of caves as well as on **3** their muzzles, ears, wing membranes, and hairless body parts. For reasons currently unknown, infected bats also demonstrate atypical behavior at

hibernation sites: they awaken, fly outside during the day, and hover around cave mouths. This excessive activity results in the depletion of vital fat stores leading to life-threatening emaciation.

A. NO CHANGE

B. its

C. bats'

D. scientists'

1. 答案

C。

2. 精讲

此题画线部分为代词，所以判定其是指代题。我们需要了解此句句意才能确定代词存在的问题到底是什么，句子意思是：科学家确定引起 white-nose syndrome 的原因是真菌，它可以在寒冷、湿润的环境中生存并且通过产生孢子繁殖，孢子寄宿在洞穴的地面、墙壁和 _____ 的口鼻、耳朵、翼膜和无毛发的身体部分。从语意上看，their 应该指代一种动物，而这句话中并没有任何表示动物的名词可以指代，所以判定此句问题是空指。空指的修改方案是把代词改为指代的名词，从上一段得知这篇文章的主题是蝙蝠，所以把 their 直接替换成 bats' 即可，所以答案选 C。

However, by the 1970s, the white paint had begun to fade, and the bright colors of the mural were beginning to show through. At the same time, a social and civil rights movement for Mexican Americans was working to raise awareness of Mexican American cultural identity. Artists associated with **7** this began to rediscover and promote the work of the Mexican muralists, particularly Siqueiros. To them, "América Tropical" was an example of how art in public spaces could be used to celebrate Mexican American heritage while at the same time making a political statement. Inspired by Siqueiros and the other muralists, this new generation of artists strove to emulate the old mural masters.

A. NO CHANGE

B. it

C. them

D. this movement

1. 答案

D。

2. 精讲

此题画线部分为指代词，所以判定是指代题。很明显，this 是想指代前一句中的单数名词，所以我们要看一下前一句的语意，确定代词指代是否正确。前一句意思是：与此同时，一场墨西哥裔美国人争取社会人权的运动正在努力提升墨西哥裔美国人的文化认同感。句中有两个单数名词 movement 和 cultural identity 可以指代，而画线部分所在句中只有一个代词，所以判定问题是指代不明，修改指代不明问题的方法是把代词指代的名词直接表达出来，所以选 D。

B. 所有格题（Possessive determiners）

题目考查考生对物主代词（如 its、your）、缩写（如 it's、you're）及副词（如 there）

进行区分的能力。

★ 题目形式

Scientists have long known that soot particles facilitate melting by darkening snow and ice, limiting **19** it's ability to reflect the Sun's rays.

A. NO CHANGE

B. its

C. there

D. their

★ 技巧真经

- 所有格题题目的画线部分通常为物主代词（如 its、your）、缩写（如 it's、you're）或副词（如 there），考生可以据此特征来判断题型。

- 此题比较简单，通过句子结构，即可分辨句子是需要用物主代词还是主谓缩写指代名词。

★ 例题

1-MCP works by limiting a fruit's production of ethylene, a chemical that causes fruit to ripen and eventually rot. While 1-MCP keeps apples firm and crisp for months, it also limits **26** their scent production. This may not be much of a problem with certain kinds of apples that are not naturally very fragrant, such as Granny Smith, but for apples that are prized for their fruity fragrance, such as McIntosh, this can be a problem with consumers, that will reject apples lacking the expected aroma.

A. NO CHANGE

B. there

C. its

D. it's

1. 答案

A。

2. 精讲

题目画线部分是物主代词 their，选项中出现了副词 there 和缩写 it's，说明此题是所有格题。此题需要通过句意判定此处是需要用物主代词还是缩写或副词。此句意思是：虽然 1-MCP 使苹果在数月中保持结实和清脆，但是它也会限制 _____ 产生香味。通过语意可知，此处需要用物主代词指代 apples，所以选择 A。

C. 一致性题（Agreement）

此题考查主谓一致原则、代词与指代名词的单复数一致原则及名词与名词的一致关系。

★ 题目形式

On the Graduate Record Examination (GRE), for example, students intending to study philosophy in graduate school 40 has scored higher than students in all but four other majors.

A. NO CHANGE

B. have scored

C. scores

D. scoring

⭐ 技巧真经

- 若题目画线部分是动词，考查主谓一致，即主语和谓语单复数一致，考生要记住两个主谓一致的原则，即就前原则和就近原则。

就前原则：主语部分有很多名词，谓语动词与最前面的名词单复数一致。

① A of B

原则：当 A of B 作主语时，核心词是 A，谓语动词单复数与 A 保持一致。

② 特殊搭配

当主语是 A with B、A as well as B、A together with B、A along with B、A rather than B 这五种情况时，谓语动词的单复数与前面的 A 保持一致。

③ S + 长串修饰语 + V

即 S + 非谓语 / 定语从句 / 介词结构 / 插入语 + V，把长串修饰语删掉，找到最前面的 S，谓语应与其保持一致。

就近原则：主语部分有很多名词，谓语动词与离自己最近的名词单复数一致。

当主语是 A or B、not A but B、either A or B、not only A but also B、neither A nor B 这五种情况时，谓语动词与离自己最近的 B 保持单复数一致。

- 若题目画线部分是代词，考查代词与指代名词的单复数一致性，考生需要通过语意判断代词指代哪个名词，通过指代名词的单复数来判断代词单复数。

注：he 或 she 只能指代单数名词，并且是不知道性别的单数名词，比如 a student、a worker、someone、one。

✪ 例题

Just as travelers taking road trips today may need to take a break for food at a rest area along the highway, settlers traversing the American West by train in the mid-1800s often found **12** themselves in need of refreshment. However, food available on rail lines was generally of terrible quality. To capitalize on the demand for good food, Fred Harvey, an English-born entrepreneur, decided to open his own restaurant business to serve rail customers. Beginning in the 1870s, he opened dozens of restaurants in rail stations and dining cars.

A. NO CHANGE

B. himself or herself

C. their selves

D. oneself

1. 答案

A。

2. 精讲

此题画线部分是代词，选项中出现了代词单复数形式的变化，所以判定此题是一致性题。我们需要通过句意了解代词到底指代哪一个名词，才能确定单复数形式哪个正确。代词所在句意思是：正像今天那些在公路上自驾的旅行者们在沿途需要休息吃东西一样，19世纪中期的那些坐火车横跨美国西部的定居者也经常发现 _____ 需要食物和点心。通过句意可知代词要指代复数名词 settlers，所以代词应该是复数，答案为 A。

> However, food available on rail lines was generally of terrible quality. To capitalize on the demand for good food, Fred Harvey, an English-born entrepreneur, decided to open his own restaurant business to serve rail customers. Beginning in the 1870s, he opened dozens of restaurants in rail stations and dining cars. These Harvey Houses, which constituted the first restaurant chain in the United States, 15 was unique for its high standards of service and quality. The menu was modeled after those of fine restaurants, so the food was leagues beyond the sinister fare travelers were accustomed to receiving in transit.
>
> A. NO CHANGE
>
> B. were unique for their
>
> C. was unique for their
>
> D. were unique for its

1. 答案

B。

2. 精讲

此题画线部分为动词和代词，选项中也出现了动词和代词的单复数变化，所以判定此题是一致性题。这时我们要想到就前原则和就近原则，根据句式结构可知，此题考查主谓一致就前原则的第三种情况"S + 长串修饰语 + V"，所以双逗号之间的插入语可以删掉，主语是 these Harvey Houses，那么谓语应该是复数，通过语意可知代词应该指代主语，也应该是复数，所以选择 B。

D. 易混词题（Frequently confused words）

题目要求区分读音相似、拼写相似的词汇，考查考生词汇记忆的准确性。

★ 题目形式

> Brice Russ of Ohio State University, for example, has employed software to sort through postings on one social media 30 cite in search of particular words and phrases of interest as well as the location from which users are posting.
>
> A. NO CHANGE
>
> B. site in search of
>
> C. sight in search for
>
> D. cite in search for

★ 技巧真经

- 易混词题目的四个选项中会出现读音相似、拼写相似的词汇，考生可以据此特征来判断题型。

- 要解此题，考生要对读音相似、拼写相似的易混词有更精准的掌握，通过句意判断答案。

高频考查易混词：

① **excess** [ɪk'ses] *n.* 过量；过度

　　access ['ækses] *v.* 接近；到达　　*n.* 通道；机会

　　assess [ə'ses] *v.* 评估

② **effect** [ɪ'fekt] *n.* 影响

　affect [ə'fekt] *v.* 影响

③ **fair** [fer] *n.* 集市；游乐园　*adj.* 公平的

　fare [fer] *n.* 费用；饭菜

④ **reduction** [rɪ'dʌkʃn] *n.* 减少

　deduction [dɪ'dʌkʃn] *n.* 演绎；推论

⑤ **principle** ['prɪnsəpl] *n.* 原则

　principal ['prɪnsəpl] *adj.* 主要的　*n.* 校长

⑥ **site** [saɪt] *n.* 地点

　cite [saɪt] *v.* 提及；引用

　sight [saɪt] *n.* 视野；景象

　recite [rɪ'saɪt] *v.* 背诵

　incite [ɪn'saɪt] *v.* 煽动

⑦ **perspire** [pər'spaɪər] *v.* 出汗

　respire [rɪ'spaɪər] *v.* 呼吸

　inspire [ɪn'spaɪər] *v.* 激发；鼓舞

　aspire [ə'spaɪər] *v.* 渴望

⑧ **ensure** [ɪn'ʃʊr] *v.* 保证；确保

assure [ə'ʃʊr] *v.* 向……保证

insure [ɪn'ʃʊr] *v.* 投保

reassure [ˌriːə'ʃʊr] *v.* 使安心

❖ 例题

More like a **38** fair then an actual café, the first Repair Café took place in Amsterdam, the Netherlands. It was the brainchild of former journalist Martine Postma, who wanted to take a practical stand in a throwaway culture. Her goals were straightforward: reduce waste, maintain and perpetuate knowledge and skills, and strengthen community. Participants bring all manner of damaged articles—clothing, appliances, furniture, and more—to be repaired by a staff of volunteer specialists including tailors, electricians, and carpenters. Since the inaugural Repair Café, others have been hosted in theater foyers, community centers, hotels, and auditoriums.

A. NO CHANGE

B. fair than

C. fare than

D. fair, then

1. 答案

B。

2. 精讲

此题的选项中出现了读音相似、拼写相似的词汇 fair 和 fare、then 和 than，由此我们判定此题是易混词题。此题需要通过语意判断需要的词义，此句前半句的语意是：更像是一个 _____ 而不是一个真正的咖啡馆。more 后面跟的必然是 than，与咖啡馆进行对比，fair 作名词意思是"集市"，fare 作名词的意思是"车费"或"食物"，而与 café 类别一致的应该是 fair，所以答案选 B。

E. 比较结构题（Logical comparison）

题目要求识别或修改比较关系中比较对象不一致的现象。

★ 题目形式

> Some people buy organic food because they believe organically grown crops are more nutritious and safer for consumption than **12** the people who purchase their conventionally grown counterparts, which are usually produced with pesticides and synthetic fertilizers.
>
> A. NO CHANGE
>
> B. the purchase of
>
> C. purchasing
>
> D. DELETE the underlined portion.

★ 技巧真经

- 比较结构题题目画线部分所在句会出现比较结构标志词，考生需要根据比较结构标志词判断题型。

- 做题时要找到比较结构的两个对象，判断两个对象的类别是否一致，若不一致，则需修改。

① 比较对象不一致的高频考查结构

a. A's dog is more…than B (应为 B's)

b. the cost of A is more…than B (应为 that of B)

② 比较结构标志词及 A、B 两个对象的准确位置

A is more…than B.

A is less…than B.

A is as…as B.

A differ from B.

A is similar to B.

like/unlike A, B…

compare A with B…

in contrast to A, B…

★ 例题

Some people buy organic food because they believe organically grown crops are more nutritious and safer for consumption than **12** the people who purchase their conventionally grown counterparts, which are usually produced with pesticides and synthetic fertilizers. In the name of health, spending $1.60 for every dollar they would have spent on food that is grown in a manner that is considered conventional. Scientific evidence, therefore, suggests that consumers do not reap significant benefits, in terms of either nutritional value or safety, from organic food.

A. NO CHANGE

B. the purchase of

C. purchasing

D. DELETE the underlined portion.

1. 答案

D。

2. 精讲

此题画线句前出现了比较结构标志词 more…than，所以我们判断此题是比较结构题。比较结构题主要考查的是比较关系中两个对象的一致性，所以我们只要找到两个对象，看它们是否一致，就能确定答案。more…than 的比较对象分别在 more 之前和 than 之后，more 之前的对象是 organically grown crops，说明 than 之后的对象也应该是 crops，因此答案选择 D，counterparts 指的就是 crops。

F. 标准搭配题（Conventional expression）

题目要求识别或修改词组搭配即名词与介词搭配、动词与介词搭配、形容词与介词搭配等出现的问题，考查考生时词组标准搭配的积累。

★ 题目形式

Nutritionists consider Greek yogurt to be a healthy food: it is an excellent source of calcium and protein, serves **7** to be a digestive aid, and it contains few calories in its unsweetened low- and non-fat forms.

A. NO CHANGE

B. as

C. like

D. for

★ 技巧真经

因为此题考查各种搭配错误，即名词与介词搭配、动词与介词搭配和形容词与介词搭配，所以选项中会体现不同的介词搭配，考生可以根据此特征来判断题型。

下面总结的是可汗学院模拟题和历年 SAT 真题考查过的词组搭配。

高频考查词组搭配汇总：

① **serve as** 充当

② **an article about** 一篇关于……的文章

③ **be amenable to** 顺从；可用某种方式处理的

④ **be integral to** 对……很重要

⑤ **be consistent with** 与……一致

⑥ **an array of** 大量的

⑦ **boycott of/on** 对……的抵制

⑧ **wrestle with** 处理（= cope with = deal with = grapple with）

⑨ **prior to** 在……之前

⑩ **connection to** 联结

⑪ **be sensitive to** 对……敏感

⑫ **be obsessed with** 迷恋

⑬ **object to** 反对

⑭ **be scheduled for** 安排在某个时间进行

⑮ **regard sth. as** 把……看成

⑯ **prefer A to B** 喜欢 A 而不是 B

⑰ **be responsible for** 对……负责任

⑱ **be helpful in** 有助于

⑲ **be particular about** 讲究；对……挑剔

⑳ **on the verge of** 将要；濒临

㉑ **have an opposition to** 反对

㉒ **be jealous of** 嫉妒（= be envious of）

㉓ **separate from** 分离（= detach from = divorce from = split off）

㉔ **liken A to B** 把 A 比作 B（= compare A to B）

㉕ **be afflicted with** 遭受

㉖ **be oblivious to** 不在意

㉗ **be partial to** 对……偏袒的

㉘ **comply with** 遵守（= abide by = conform to）

㉙ **succeed in doing** 成功完成（= manage to do）

㉚ **be capable of** 有能力做

㉛ **be pertinent to** 与……有关（= be related to）

㉜ **be desirous of** 渴望

㉝ **compare A with B** 把 A 和 B 做比较

㉞ **be suitable for** 适合于

㉟ **attempt to do sth.** 尝试做某事

㊱ **give in to sth.** 屈服于某事（= yield to = submit to = succumb to）

㊲ **in the aftermath of** 在……之后

㊳ **claim to do sth.** 声称做某事

㊴ **desire for sth./desire to do sth.** 渴望做某事（= yearn for sth./yearn to do sth. = long for sth./long to do sth. = be eager for sth./be eager to do sth.）

㊵ **attach to** 依附

㊶ **be resistant to** 抵抗

㊷ **be liable to** 易于（= be apt to）

㊸ **be prone to** 倾向于（= tend to = be inclined to = be likely to）

㊹ **subject to** 遭受

㊺ **distinguish from** 区分（= differentiate from = discriminate from = tell from）

㊻ **have a reputation for** 以……闻名

㊼ **attest to** 证实

㊽ **integrate into** 融入

㊾ **lean on** 依靠（= count on = rest on = rely on = depend on）

㊿ **in times of** 在……的时候

(51) **a means/method of** 一种……的方法

(52) **be notorious for** 因……臭名昭著

(53) **approach to** 接近

(54) **be lacking in＝in lack of** 缺乏

(55) **be acclaimed as** 被誉为

(56) **have grounds for** 有……的理由

(57) **model after** 仿照；模仿

(58) **be termed as** 被叫作

(59) **be deficient in** 缺乏（= be devoid of = be short of）

(60) **on the grounds of** 基于

(61) **in pursuit of** 追求

(62) **in search of** 寻找

(63) **be criticized for** 因为……受批评

(64) **have an edge over** 比……占优势

(65) **apply to** 应用

例题

Among the possibilities to reconfigure a building's lighting is the installation of full-pane windows to allow the greatest degree of sunlight to reach office interiors. Alternatively, businesses can install light tubes, which are pipes placed in workplace roofs to capture and funnel sunlight down into a building's interior. Glass walls and dividers can also be used to replace solid walls as a means **11** through distributing natural light more freely. Considering the enormous costs of artificial lighting, both in terms of money and productivity, investment in such improvements should be a natural choice for businesses.

A. NO CHANGE

B. of

C. from

D. DELETE the underlined portion.

1. 答案

B。

2. 精讲

此题画线部分是介词，所以判断此题是标准搭配题。此题考查 means 的介词搭配，在表示"方法"的词汇中，way/solution/measure 后面跟介词 to，means/method 后面跟介词 of，remedy 后面跟介词 for，所以答案选择 B。

三、标准符号题（Conventions of Punctuation）

A. 句末符号题（End-of-sentence punctuation）

题目要求识别句末符号如句号、叹号和问号的使用是否恰当。

★ 题目形式

> For example, experts still do not know what long-term impacts the hospitalist movement will have on the general internist and family medicine **9** workforce?
>
> A. NO CHANGE
> B. workforce;
> C. workforce!
> D. workforce.

★ 技巧真经

- 选项中出现句号、问号或叹号的变化时，考生可以判断此题是句末符号题。

- 大部分考生对句末符号的掌握还是不错的，所以 SAT 文法考试在这类题型中只会考查一种情况，即间接疑问句。举个例子，直接疑问句 He asked, "Is it raining?" 改为间接疑问句是：He asked if it is raining. 考生们只要记住间接疑问句应该以句号结尾即可。

★ 例题

> For example, experts still do not know what long-term impacts the hospitalist movement will have on the general internist and family medicine **9** workforce?
>
> A. NO CHANGE
>
> B. workforce;
>
> C. workforce!
>
> D. workforce.

1. 答案

D。

2. 精讲

选项中出现了问号、句号和叹号的变化，说明此题考查句末符号。这句话就是一个间接疑问句，应该用句号结尾，所以选择 D。

B. 句中符号题（Within-sentence punctuation）

题目要求识别分号、冒号和破折号的用法是否恰当。

第四章 标准语法类题目（Standard English Conventions）技巧真经

★ 题目形式

I liked the experience so much that I now go to the co-working space a few times a week. Over time, I've gotten to know several of my co-working **32** colleagues: another website developer, a graphic designer, a freelance writer, and several mobile app coders.

A. NO CHANGE

B. colleagues;

C. colleagues,

D. colleagues

★ 技巧真经

- 第一，句中符号题会考查分号的用法，考生们要记住分号是要连接两个并列的、联系非常紧密的独立句。

- 第二，句中符号题会考查同位语符号的用法，同位语符号有逗号、破折号和冒号三种，同位语形式如下：

1) N, S + V + O（同位语 N 解释主语内容）

2) S + V + O—N/S + V + O: N（同位语 N 解释宾语或主语内容）

3) S + V + O: S + V + O/S + V + O—S + V + O（冒号和破折号后面的句子是同位语，解释前面整个主句的内容）

考生们要记住这三种同位语的句式结构，若题目句子符合这三种句式，要根据这三种句式的符号判断正误。

✯ 例题

Not all research into regional English varieties requires such time, effort, and resources, however. Today's researchers have found that the veritable army of trained volunteers traveling the country conducting face-to-face interviews can sometimes be 29 replaced by another army the vast array of individuals volunteering details about their lives—and, inadvertently, their language—through social media. Brice Russ of Ohio State University, for example, has employed software to sort through postings on one social media cite in search of particular words and phrases of interest as well as the location from which users are posting.

A. NO CHANGE

B. replaced—by another army,

C. replaced by another army;

D. replaced by another army:

1. 答案

D。

2. 精讲

此题的四个选项有不同的符号变化，由此可以判断此题是标准符号题，这个句子到底需要怎样的符号，我们要通过句意和句子结构来判断。该句意为：今天的研究者们发现那些经过培训、去各个国家进行面对面采访的大批志愿者正在被另外一群人取代，一大群通过社交媒体主动提供自己信息的个体。通过语意可知，"the vast array of individuals volunteering details about their lives—and, inadvertently, their language—through social media" 这部分内容是在解释 another army，所以此处需要同位语的符号，而此句句式符合同位语的第二种形式 "S + V + O—N/S + V + O: N"，因此答案选择 D。

C. 名词所有格&代词所有格题（Possessive nouns and pronouns）

题目要求识别和修改名词所有格和物主代词使用不恰当的问题。

☆ 题目形式

Circadian rhythms, which are controlled by the **4** bodies biological clocks, influence body temperature, hormone release, cycles of sleep and wakefulness, and other bodily functions. Disruptions of circadian rhythms have been linked to sleep disorders, diabetes, depression, and bipolar disorder.

A. NO CHANGE

B. bodies' biological clocks',

C. body's biological clocks,

D. body's biological clock's,

☆ 技巧真经

名词所有格和物主代词使用不恰当的情况经常出现在单复数的所有格的变化上，考生要通过语意判断句子到底是需要单数名词所有格还是复数名词所有格，再进行相应的变化。

☆ 例题

If a petroleum engineer is able to contribute to an increase in this rate of just a fraction of a percentage, it can mean millions of additional barrels of oil; however, the demand for the expertise of a petroleum engineer is understandable. Further, a petroleum **8** engineers skills' are applicable to areas beyond oil exploration. Petroleum engineers also commonly work in pollution cleanup, underground waste disposal, and water resource management.

A. NO CHANGE

B. engineer's skills

C. engineers' skills

D. engineers skill's

1. 答案

B.

2. 精讲

四个选项中出现了单复数名词所有格的变化，所以判断此题是名词所有格题。此题需要我们通过句意判断是否需要名词所有格和名词所有格的单复数状态，句中有冠词 a，所以确定 engineer 应该是单数，通过句子结构，我们确定 skills 是主语，不需要变成所有格形式，所以答案选择 B。

D. 并列符号题（Items in a series）

题目要求识别和修改并列符号","和";"使用不恰当的问题。

★ 题目形式

Yogurt manufacturers, food **4** scientists; and government officials are also working together to develop additional solutions for reusing whey.

A. NO CHANGE

B. scientists: and

C. scientists, and

D. scientists, and,

⭐ 技巧真经

- 逗号可以连接并列的单词、词组或从句，但绝不能连接并列的句子。并列成分在两个以上才需要用逗号，并列的形式有"A, B, and C"或"A, B and C"，也就是说，B 成分后面的逗号可加可不加，取决于并列成分的长短。如果并列成分比较长，可以在 B 后加上逗号，目的是让读者停顿一下；如果并列成分比较短，B 后就不需要加逗号进行停顿。

- 分号可以连接并列的句子，不能连接并列的单词、词组和从句。并列形式：S1 + V1 + O1; S2 + V2 + O2; S3 + V3 + O3.

⭐ 例题

In 1925, Hurston began her studies at Barnard College, where, under the tutelage of Franz Boas, the "Father of Modern Anthropology"—she embraced the idea of cultural relativism, or studying a culture in isolation rather than in comparison to others. Her work reflected this exposition, as she sought to capture what she termed the "natural" art of African Americans 6 through speech song and folklore. By adopting the vernacular, for example, Hurston believed that she could develop the authenticity of her characters and present the uniqueness of African American culture.

A. NO CHANGE

B. through speech, song, and, folklore.

C. through: speech, song, and folklore.

D. through speech, song, and folklore.

1. 答案

D。

2. 精讲

此题的四个选项有不同的符号，可以判断此题是标准符号题，句子到底需要怎样的符号，我们要通过句意和句子结构来判断。此题用 through 引导方式状语，后面形成了三个名词的并列，通过技巧的学习，我们知道并列的单词需要用逗号连接，正确形式有两种 "A, B, and C" 或 "A, B and C"，所以答案选择 D。

E. 插入符号题（Nonrestrictive and parenthetical elements）

题目要求考生掌握不重要的插入成分，如插入语的符号使用。

☆ 题目形式

In the Bakken [6] formation, a highly productive oil field located in North Dakota only 3.5 percent of the oil deposits in the rock are currently recovered.

A. NO CHANGE

B. formation a highly productive oil field located in North Dakota

C. formation, a highly productive oil field located in North Dakota,

D. formation a highly productive oil field located in North Dakota,

☆ 技巧真经

- 引导插入语的符号有两种，一种是双逗号，一种是双破折号。无论是逗号还是破折号，都是成对出现，因此在考查插入语符号时，题目中经常只出现一部分符号，即一个逗号或一个破折号，这种情况就可以判断为错误。

⭐ 例题

If you love video games and have thought about how the games you play might be changed or improved, or if you've imagined creating a video game of your own, you might want to consider a career as a video game designer. There were a number of steps you can take to determine whether game design is the right field for you and, if it is, to prepare yourself for such a career. Before making the choice, you should have some sense of what a video game designer does. Every video game, whether for a console, computer, or mobile device, starts with a concept that originates in the mind of a designer. The designer envisions the game's fundamental **35** <u>elements: the settings, characters, and plots that make each game unique,</u> and is thus a primary creative force behind a video game.

A. NO CHANGE

B. elements: the settings, characters, and plots that make each game unique—

C. elements—the settings, characters, and plots that make each game unique—

D. elements; the settings, characters, and plots that make each game unique;

1. 答案

C。

2. 精讲

此题的四个选项有不同的符号变化，由此可以判断此题是标准符号题，这个句子到底需要怎样的符号，我们要通过句意和句子结构来判断。本句意为：设计师会想象游戏的基本元素，如背景、角色和情节，因此是电子游戏背后主要的创造力量。句中的"the settings, characters, and plots that make each game unique"应该是在解释elements，所以

elements 后需要同位语符号。首先排除 D 选项，因为 D 选项 elements 后是分号；A 选项 elements 后面是冒号，但是 unique 后是逗号，会让读者以为 and 前后的部分 "the settings, characters, and plots that make each game unique" 和 "is thus a primary creative force behind a video game" 并列，但是这两部分内容完全不平行，所以是错误的；B 选项 unique 后面是破折号，表示破折号后面的内容在解释前面的内容，但语意上并非如此，所以是错误的；C 选项用了双破折号，构成了插入语，and 前后两个句子并列，结构也正确。

F. 多余符号题（Unnecessary punctuation）

题目要求识别和修改没必要使用的符号。

★ 题目形式

The article, published by *Forbes* magazine, explained that coworking spaces are designated locations that, for a fee, individuals can use to conduct their work. The spaces are usually stocked with standard office 26 equipment, such as photocopiers, printers, and fax machines.

A. NO CHANGE

B. equipment, such as:

C. equipment such as:

D. equipment, such as,

★ 技巧真经

● 在题目中，没必要使用的符号经常出现在修饰语与名词之间（如 "A, of B" 的正确形式为 "A of B"）、主语和谓语之间（如 "S, V + O" 的正确形式为 "S + V + O"）、谓语与宾语之间（如 "I suggest, that S + V + O" 的正确形式为 "I suggest that S + V + O"）或者一些固定表达中（如 "S + V + O, such as: A, B and C" 的正确形式为 "S + V + O, such as A, B and C"）。过多的符号会减缓读者的阅读速度并且给读者造成困扰，所以在出现以上几种符号多余的情况时，请考生们一定要注意。

★ 例题

Based on scientific evidence, organic food offers neither significant nutritional nor safety benefits for consumers. Proponents of organic food, of course, are quick to add that there are numerous other reasons to buy organic 22 food, such as, a desire to protect the environment from potentially damaging pesticides or a preference for the taste of organically grown foods. Research regarding these issues is less conclusive than the findings regarding nutritional content and pesticide residue safety limits. What is clear, though, is this: if a consumer's goal is to buy the healthiest and safest food to eat, the increased cost of organic food is a waste of money.

A. NO CHANGE

B. food such as:

C. food such as,

D. food, such as

1. 答案

D。

2. 精讲

此题的四个选项有不同的符号变化，可以据此判断此题是标准符号题，到底句子需要怎样的符号，我们要通过句意和句子结构来判断。此题考查 such as 的符号用法，通过前面的技巧讲解，我们应该知道正确用法是"S + V + O, such as A, B and C"，A、B、C 三个选项都在 such as 后面加上了多余的符号，所以答案是 D。

第五章

历史/社会研究类
文章真题精讲

Writing and Language Test

35 MINUTES, 44 QUESTIONS

Turn to Section 2 of your answer sheet to answer the questions in this section.

DIRECTIONS

Each passage below is accompanied by a number of questions. For some questions, you will consider how the passage might be revised to improve the expression of ideas. For other questions, you will consider how the passage might be edited to correct errors in sentence structure, usage, or punctuation. A passage or a question may be accompanied by one or more graphics (such as a table or graph) that you will consider as you make revising and editing decisions.

Some questions will direct you to an underlined portion of a passage. Other questions will direct you to a location in a passage or ask you to think about the passage as a whole.

After reading each passage, choose the answer to each question that most effectively improves the quality of writing in the passage or that makes the passage conform to the conventions of standard written English. Many questions include a "NO CHANGE" option. Choose that option if you think the best choice is to leave the relevant portion of the passage as it is.

Questions 1–11 are based on the following passage.

Whey to Go

Greek yogurt—a strained form of cultured yogurt—has grown enormously in popularity in the United States since it was first introduced in the country in the late 1980s.

From 2011 to 2012 alone, sales of Greek yogurt in the US increased by 50 percent. The resulting increase in Greek yogurt production has forced those involved in the business to address the detrimental effects that the yogurt-making process may be having on the environment. Fortunately, farmers and others in the Greek yogurt business have found many methods of controlling and eliminating most environmental threats. Given these solutions as well as the many health benefits of the food, the advantages of Greek yogurt [1] outdo the potential drawbacks of its production.

1

A. NO CHANGE

B. defeat

C. outperform

D. outweigh

[1] The main environmental problem caused by the production of Greek yogurt is the creation of acid whey as a by-product. [2] Because it requires up to four times more milk to make than conventional yogurt does, Greek yogurt produces larger amounts of acid whey, which is difficult to dispose of. [3] To address the problem of disposal, farmers have found a number of uses for acid whey. [4] They can add it to livestock feed as a protein **2** supplement, and people can make their own Greek-style yogurt at home by straining regular yogurt. [5] If it is improperly introduced into the environment, acid-whey runoff **3** can pollute waterways, depleting the oxygen content of streams and rivers as it decomposes. [6] Yogurt manufacturers, food **4** scientists; and government officials are also working together to develop additional solutions for reusing whey. **5**

2

Which choice provides the most relevant detail?

A. NO CHANGE

B. supplement and convert it into gas to use as fuel in electricity production.

C. supplement, while sweet whey is more desirable as a food additive for humans.

D. supplement, which provides an important element of their diet.

3

A. NO CHANGE

B. can pollute waterway's,

C. could have polluted waterways,

D. has polluted waterway's,

4

A. NO CHANGE

B. scientists: and

C. scientists, and

D. scientists, and,

5

To make this paragraph most logical, sentence 5 should be placed

A. where it is now.

B. after sentence 1.

C. after sentence 2.

D. after sentence 3.

[6] Though these conservation methods can be costly and time-consuming, they are well worth the effort. Nutritionists consider Greek yogurt to be a healthy food: it is an excellent source of calcium and protein, serves [7] to be a digestive aid, and [8] it contains few calories in its unsweetened low- and non-fat forms.

6

The writer is considering deleting the underlined sentence. Should the writer do this?

A. Yes, because it does not provide a transition from the previous paragraph.

B. Yes, because it fails to support the main argument of the passage as introduced in the first paragraph.

C. No, because it continues the explanation of how acid whey can be disposed of safely.

D. No, because it sets up the argument in the paragraph for the benefits of Greek yogurt.

7

A. NO CHANGE

B. as

C. like

D. for

8

A. NO CHANGE

B. containing

C. contains

D. will contain

Greek yogurt is slightly lower in sugar and carbohydrates than conventional yogurt is. [9] Also, because it is more concentrated, Greek yogurt contains slightly more protein per serving, thereby helping people stay [10] satiated for longer periods of time. These health benefits have prompted Greek yogurt's recent surge in popularity. In fact, Greek yogurt can be found in an increasing number of products such as snack food and frozen desserts. Because consumers reap the nutritional benefits of Greek yogurt and support those who make and sell [11] it, therefore farmers and businesses should continue finding safe and effective methods of producing the food.

9

A. NO CHANGE
B. In other words,
C. Therefore,
D. For instance,

10

A. NO CHANGE
B. fulfilled
C. complacent
D. sufficient

11

A. NO CHANGE
B. it, farmers
C. it, so farmers
D. it: farmers

★ 真经派精讲

Question 1

A. NO CHANGE

B. defeat

C. outperform

D. outweigh

1. 答案

D。

2. 精讲

措辞题。outweigh 是"超过"的意思。文章中画线部分所在句的意思是：希腊酸奶的优势要大于它的生产中存在的潜在的缺点。outdo、defeat 和 outperform 都有"胜于"的意思，但是这三个词主要用于表述两个对象之间的胜负，而不是优势和劣势的比较，所以 outweigh 的意思最为准确。

Question 2

Which choice provides the most relevant detail?

A. NO CHANGE

B. supplement and convert it into gas to use as fuel in electricity production.

C. supplement, while sweet whey is more desirable as a food additive for humans.

D. supplement, which provides an important element of their diet.

1. 答案

B。

2. 精讲

论据题。原文的总说句是画线句的前一句，意思是"为了解决处理的问题，农场主们已经找到了许多应用酸乳清的方法"，由此我们可以预测下面的例子会说农场主们都找到了哪些应用酸乳清的方法。正确答案是 B 选项，其中 and 连接并列句，后半句所说的应用方法是把酸乳清转化成气体作为燃料用于电力生产。A 选项是说人们可以通过过滤常规的酸奶，在家里制作自己的希腊式酸奶；C 选项说的是甜乳清对于人类来说是更好的食品添加剂；D 选项是用 which 引导的定语从句修饰前面的 protein supplement（蛋白质补充物），说它是牲畜饲料中很重要的组成元素。这三个选项都没有举例解释总说句中提及的应用方法，所以错误。

Question 3

A. NO CHANGE

B. can pollute waterway's,

C. could have polluted waterways,

D. has polluted waterway's,

1. 答案

A。

2. 精讲

时态题。这道题考查的是 if 引导的条件状语从句的时态，"If it is..."是一般现在时，主句可以用一般将来时表示某事很可能发生，也可以用情态动词（can/may）表示某事可能会发生。A 选项的时态完全符合原文；B 选项的时态符合，但是使用了所有格 waterway's，错误；C 选项的时态是虚拟语气所用的时态，跟原文从句不符；D 选项的时态是现在完成时，这不是条件句需要的时态，所以错误。

Question 4

A. NO CHANGE

B. scientists: and

C. scientists, and

D. scientists, and,

1. 答案

C。

2. 精讲

并列符号题。这道题考查的是三个名词之间的并列，三个词分别是 yogurt manufacturers、food scientists 和 government officials，三个词并列时所用的符号应该是 "A, B and C" 或 "A, B, and C"，所以 C 选项正确。A 选项和 B 选项分别在 food scientists 后加了分号和冒号，这是错误的；D 选项在 and 后面加了逗号，是没有必要的符号，所以错误。

Question 5

To make this paragraph most logical, sentence 5 should be placed

A. where it is now.

B. after sentence 1.

C. after sentence 2.

D. after sentence 3.

1. 答案

C。

2. 精讲

逻辑顺序题。这道题考查的是句子与句子之间的逻辑，所用我们要先判断插入句子的逻辑。从 sentence 5 的句式结构能判断出它是主谓宾逻辑，句式结构是靠逗号隔开前后半句，所以前半句可以跟前一句承接，后半句可以跟后一句承接。前半句讲的是"如果酸乳清被不恰当地排放到环境中"，所以文章前一句讲的也应该是酸乳清处理不恰当的事情，后半句讲的是"酸乳清会污染水域，消耗小溪和河流的氧成分"，所以文章后一句也应该讲酸乳清对环境的污染和破坏问题，符合这种预测的是 C 选项，即放在第 2 句后面，第 2 句讲的是希腊酸奶会产生大量的酸乳清，很难处理，第 3 句说的则是为了解决这个问题，农场主找到了许多应用方法，与酸乳清处理后对环境的污染问题承接，所以答案正确。

错误选项：A 选项是放在第 4 和第 6 句之间，联系第 2 题可知，第 4 句讲的是农场主为解决问题所做的一些努力，与第 5 句前半句的预测不符；B 选项是放在第 1 和第 2 句之间，第 1 句讲的是希腊酸奶引发的环境问题是会产生酸乳清这种副产品，与我们的预测不符；D 选项是放在第 3 和第 4 句之间，第 3 句讲的是为解决处理的问题，农场主找到了很多应用酸乳清的方法，与我们的预测不符。

Question 6

The writer is considering deleting the underlined sentence. Should the writer do this?

A. Yes, because it does not provide a transition from the previous paragraph.

B. Yes, because it fails to support the main argument of the passage as introduced in the first paragraph.

C. No, because it continues the explanation of how acid whey can be disposed of safely.

D. No, because it sets up the argument in the paragraph for the benefits of Greek yogurt.

1. 答案

D。

2. 精讲

焦点题。当焦点题中问某个句子是否可以删减时，考生要考虑的是这个句子与前后句的关系是否紧密，若逻辑紧密，则不能删减，若无关系，则可删减。这句话被逗号隔开前后半句，那么前半句应该与前文承接，后半句应与后文承接。前半句中出现指代逻辑 these conservation methods，说明前文应该说到了很多保护措施，通过前面的题目可知上一段的主要内容就是因为酸乳清很难处理，所以人们想出了很多方法利用酸乳清进而保护环境，所以说明两部分内容是前后承接的；后半句说的是这些费钱费时的保护方法是很值得的，而下文则说希腊酸奶是一种健康食品，所以也是符合逻辑的。因此，这句话与前后文的关系都很紧密，不能删减，于是可以排除 A、B 选项。C 选项说这句话继续解释了如何安全地处理酸乳清，内容概括错误，排除；D 选项说这句话建立了本段的论点，说明了希腊酸奶的益处，这是正确的。

> **Question 7**
>
> A. NO CHANGE
>
> B. as
>
> C. like
>
> D. for

1. 答案

B。

2. 精讲

标准搭配题。此题考查的是 serve as 这个固定搭配，直接选择即可，serve 与其他三个介词都无法搭配。

Question 8

  A. NO CHANGE

  B. containing

  C. contains

  D. will contain

1. 答案

C。

2. 精讲

平行结构题。通过 and 这个平行结构标志词判断这道题考查平行结构，接下来就要分析句子结构来判断 and 连接的并列成分。通过分析可知这句话中并列的是动词，前两个动词分别是 is 和 serves，时态是一般现在时，而且是单数形式，所以第三个动词也必须符合以上要求，所以选择 C；A 选项不是动词的并列，错误；B 选项是动词的 -ing 形式，与平行结构不符；D 选项时态错误。

Question 9

  A. NO CHANGE

  B. In other words,

  C. Therefore,

  D. For instance,

1. 答案

A。

2. 精讲

开篇句 & 结论句 & 过渡句题。此题考查前后两句话的逻辑过渡词，我们需要了解两句话的语意之后再判断两句话的逻辑关系。前一句话的意思是"希腊酸奶比传统酸奶的糖分和碳水化合物含量更低"，后一句的意思是"因为希腊酸奶更浓缩，所以它每一份中含有的蛋白质就会更多一些，可以帮助人们保持更长时间的饱腹感"。我们发现这两句话都是在讲希腊酸奶的益处，所以应该是并列的关系，A 选项正确；B 选项是"换句话说"，表示第二句话和第一句话的意思一致，所以错误；C 选项是"因此"，表示两句话是因果关系，而这两句话之间并没有这种逻辑关系，所以错误；D 选项是"例如"，表示第二句是对第一句进行举例说明，这并不符合原文，所以错误。

Question 10

    A. NO CHANGE

    B. fulfilled

    C. complacent

    D. sufficient

1. 答案

A。

2. 精讲

措辞题。这道题考查词与词之间的释义区别，这句话是说每一份希腊酸奶的蛋白质含量更多，可以让人们更有饱腹感，只有 satiated（充分满足的）一词符合句意；B 选项 fulfilled 表示精神上的一种成就感和满足感；C 选项 complacent 意思是"自满的，自鸣得意的"；D 选项 sufficient 是指物质很充足。

Question 11

A. NO CHANGE

B. it, farmers

C. it, so farmers

D. it: farmers

1. 答案

B。

2. 精讲

简洁性题。这道题考查重复性问题，A 选项中的 therefore 和句首的 because 语意重复，不能连用；C 选项中的 so 和句首的 because 语意重复；D 选项符号有误，原因状语从句和主句之间应该用逗号隔开，而不是冒号。

第六章

科学类文章真题精讲

Questions 12–22 are based on the following passage and supplementary material.

Dark Snow

Most of Greenland's interior is covered by a thick layer of ice and compressed snow known as the Greenland Ice Sheet. The size of the ice sheet fluctuates seasonally: in summer, average daily high temperatures in Greenland can rise to slightly above 50 degrees Fahrenheit, partially melting the ice; in the winter, the sheet thickens as additional snow falls, and average daily low temperatures can drop [12] to as low as 20 degrees.

12

Which choice most accurately and effectively represents the information in the graph?

A. NO CHANGE
B. to 12 degrees Fahrenheit.
C. to their lowest point on December 13.
D. to 10 degrees Fahrenheit and stay there for months.

Average Daily High and Low Temperatures Recorded at Nuuk Weather Station, Greenland (1961—1990)

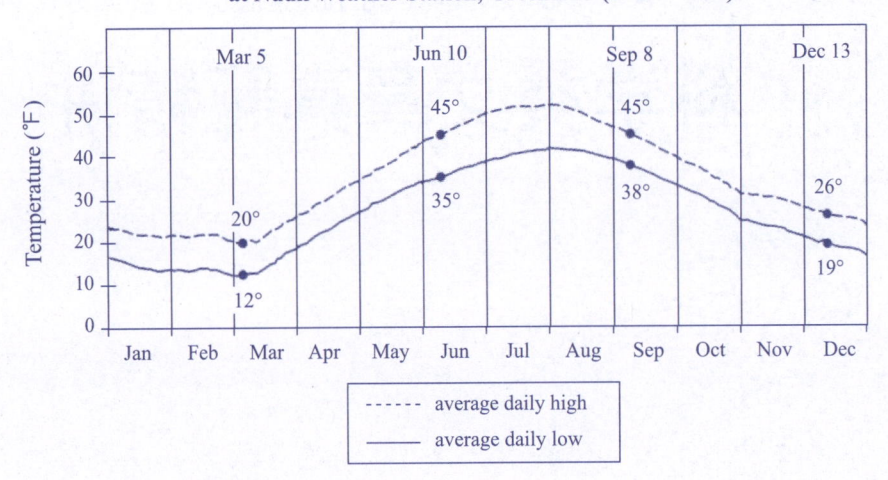

Adapted from WMO. ©2014 by World Meteorological Organization.

Typically, the ice sheet begins to show evidence of thawing in late **13** summer. This follows several weeks of higher temperatures. **14** For example, in the summer of 2012, virtually the entire Greenland Ice Sheet underwent thawing at or near its surface by mid-July, the earliest date on record. Most scientists looking for the causes of the Great Melt of 2012 have focused exclusively on rising temperatures. The summer of 2012 was the warmest in 170 years, records show. But Jason **15** Box, an associate professor of geology at Ohio State believes that another factor added to the early **16** thaw; the "dark snow" problem.

13

Which choice most effectively combines the two sentences at the underlined portion?

A. summer, following

B. summer, and this thawing follows

C. summer, and such thawing follows

D. summer and this evidence follows

14

A. NO CHANGE

B. However,

C. As such,

D. Moreover,

15

A. NO CHANGE

B. Box an associate professor of geology at Ohio State,

C. Box, an associate professor of geology at Ohio State,

D. Box, an associate professor of geology, at Ohio State

16

A. NO CHANGE

B. thaw; and it was

C. thaw:

D. thaw: being

According to Box, a leading Greenland expert, tundra fires in 2012 from as far away as North America produced great amounts of soot, some **17** of it drifted over Greenland in giant plumes of smoke and then **18** fell as particles onto the ice sheet. Scientists have long known that soot particles facilitate melting by darkening snow and ice, limiting **19** it's ability to reflect the Sun's rays. As Box explains, "Soot is an extremely powerful light absorber. It settles over the ice and captures the Sun's heat." The result is a self-reinforcing cycle. As the ice melts, the land and water under the ice become exposed, and since land and water are darker than snow, the surface absorbs even more heat, which **20** is related to the rising temperatures.

17

A. NO CHANGE

B. soot

C. of which

D. DELETE the underlined portion.

18

A. NO CHANGE

B. falls

C. will fall

D. had fallen

19

A. NO CHANGE

B. its

C. there

D. their

20

Which choice best completes the description of a self-reinforcing cycle?

A. NO CHANGE

B. raises the surface temperature.

C. begins to cool at a certain point.

D. leads to additional melting.

[1] Box's research is important because the fires of 2012 may not be a one-time phenomenon. [2] According to scientists, rising Arctic temperatures are making northern latitudes greener and thus more fire prone. [3] The pattern Box observed in 2012 may repeat **21** itself again, with harmful effects on the Arctic ecosystem. [4] Box is currently organizing an expedition to gather this crucial information. [5] The next step for Box and his team is to travel to Greenland to perform direct sampling of the ice in order to determine just how much the soot is contributing to the melting of the ice sheet. [6] Members of the public will be able to track his team's progress—and even help fund the expedition—through a website Box has created. **22**

21

A. NO CHANGE

B. itself,

C. itself, with damage and

D. itself possibly,

22

To make this paragraph most logical, sentence 4 should be placed

A. where it is now.

B. after sentence 1.

C. after sentence 2.

D. after sentence 5.

⭐ 真经派精讲

Question 12

Which choice most accurately and effectively represents the information in the graph?

A. NO CHANGE

B. to 12 degrees Fahrenheit.

C. to their lowest point on December 13.

D. to 10 degrees Fahrenheit and stay there for months.

1. 答案

B。

2. 精讲

数据信息题。数据信息题要求正确答案必须同时符合两个要求，一是要符合句意逻辑，二是要符合图表信息。首先，我们来看画线部分所在句子的语意："冰盖的大小随季节变化：在夏天，格陵兰日平均最高气温会上升到50华氏度以上，部分冰会融化；在冬天，冰盖会因为下雪而变厚，日平均最低气温会降低到_____"。通过语意，我们得知正确答案必须涉及冬天日平均最低气温的具体数值，与夏天的50华氏度形成对应。然后，我们需要在图表中找到冬天日平均最低气温的数值，看图可知，最低温度为12华氏度，所以选项B正确。A选项不是最低气温数值，所以错误；C选项中的12月13日并没有达到最低气温的数值，错误；D选项说最低气温数值是10华氏度，也是错误的。

Question 13

Which choice most effectively combines the two sentences at the underlined portion?

A. summer, following

B. summer, and this thawing follows

C. summer, and such thawing follows

D. summer and this evidence follows

1. 答案

A。

2. 精讲

句法题。句子合并后要符合两个要求：第一，两个句子之间的逻辑连接要正确；第二，句子要简洁。我们来看两句话的句意，第一句意思是：通常来说，冰盖会在夏末开始显示出融化的迹象；第二句意思是：这跟随着几周的高温。很明显两句话之间是承接性逻辑，所以 A 选项正确，following 引导伴随状语，完美地诠释了承接性逻辑；B、C、D 三个选项虽然都是 and 引导的承接性逻辑，但是都不够简洁，所以错误。

Question 14

A. NO CHANGE

B. However,

C. As such,

D. Moreover,

1. 答案

B。

2. 精讲

开篇句 & 结论句 & 过渡句题。两句之间要加一个过渡的逻辑副词，我们要通过理解前后两句的句意做出选择。前一句意思是：通常来说，冰盖会在夏末开始显示出融化的迹象；后一句意思是：在 2012 年的夏天，几乎所有的格陵兰冰盖都在七月中期就开始融化，这是有记录以来最早的时间。前后句形成了时间上早晚之间的对比，所以需要用转折词来过渡，因此 B 选项正确；A 选项是举例逻辑，表示后一句在解释前一句的内容，并不符合两句的关系；C 选项是比较逻辑，as such 是"像这种情况一样"，说明前后句是类似的情况，不符合原文；D 选项是并列逻辑，说明前后句的语意方向是一致的，也不符合原文。

Question 15

A. NO CHANGE

B. Box an associate professor of geology at Ohio State,

C. Box, an associate professor of geology at Ohio State,

D. Box, an associate professor of geology, at Ohio State

---

1. 答案

C。

2. 精讲

插入符号题。此题考查插入语的符号，应为双逗号或双破折号，句中想用 an associate professor of geology at Ohio State 去解释 Jason Box 的身份，所以这个解释的部分前后都要有逗号，所以选 C。A 选项是后面缺逗号；B 选项是前面缺逗号；D 选项的逗号放错了位置，at Ohio State 是介词短语作后置定语，这时名词和介词短语之间不需要用逗号隔开。

Question 16

A. NO CHANGE

B. thaw; and it was

C. thaw:

D. thaw: being

1. 答案

C。

2. 精讲

句中符号题。此题考查的是同位语的符号，应为逗号、破折号或冒号。句中的 the "dark snow" problem 很明显是解释前句话中的 another factor，所以可确定是同位语。满足同位语符号要求的是 C、D 两个选项，D 选项中的 being 是累赘表达，不简洁，所以选择 C 选项；A 选项中的分号前后并列的应是两个完整的句子，而原文中只是一个名词，所以错误；B 选项表达方式不简洁，是错误的。

Question 17

A. NO CHANGE

B. soot

C. of which

D. DELETE the underlined portion.

1. 答案

C。

2. 精讲

句子边界题。此题考查连排句。我们来分析一下原句结构，"According to Box" 是状语，"tundra fires…amounts of soot" 是一个完整的句子，"some of it drifted…ice sheet" 也是一个完整的句子，两个完整的句子之间不能用逗号连接，所以 A、B、D 三个选项都是错误的，因为 B 选项把主语变成 some soot，D 选项把主语变成 some，结果都和 A 选项一样，还是用逗号连接了两个句子。而 C 选项用 which 引导定语从句修饰 soot，这样就不是连排句了，所以正确。

Question 18

A. NO CHANGE

B. falls

C. will fall

D. had fallen

1. 答案

A。

2. 精讲

时态题。时态要通过语意或句子中的时间标志词来判断，本题的时间标志词是 2012，表明时态是过去时，另外，drifted 和 fell 两个谓语动词并列，有 then 连接，有时间顺序，所以应该用过去时 fell，A 选项正确。B 选项是一般现在时；C 选项是将来时；D 选项是过去完成时，都不符合时态要求，所以是错误的。

Question 19

A. NO CHANGE

B. its

C. there

D. their

1. 答案

D。

2. 精讲

所有格题。我们先来分析句子结构："Scientists have long known…by darkening snow and ice"是主句，"limiting…reflect the Sun's rays"是伴随状语，limit 是动词，后面要接一个宾语成分，所以 19 题画线部分应该填一个代词所有格修饰 ability。it's 是 it is 的省略形式，引导一个完整的句子，不能放在 limiting 后面，所以 A 选项错误；C 选项 there 是副词，所以错误；B 选项虽然是代词所有格，但是代词和指代的名词要单复数一致，通过句意我们知道这个代词应该指代 soot particles，所以 its 单复数形式错误；D 选项 their 既是代词所有格，又是复数代词，所以正确。

Question 20

Which choice best completes the description of a self-reinforcing cycle?

A. NO CHANGE

B. raises the surface temperature.

C. begins to cool at a certain point.

D. leads to additional melting.

1. 答案

D。

2. 精讲

论据题。这道题要求考生补充一部分句子的内容，使这个句子符合前一句话的描述：The result is a self-reinforcing cycle. 这两句话是总分关系，那么也就是说，考生需要把论据内容补充完整来支持总说句的内容。所以，考生首先要看总说句的内容，基于总分之间存在的语意一致性原则，通过总说句的意思去判断分说句的内容。本题总说句说的是：结果是一个自我强化的循环。既然是一个循环，那就意味着分说句在解释的时候要描述一个 A → B → C → D → A 的过程，也就是说这个自我强化过程从 A 出发，最终还要循环至 A。分说句讲到当冰融化的时候（A），冰下的土地和水暴露出来（B），因为土地和水比雪颜色更深（C），表面会吸收更多的热量（D），而最后半句话一定要回归至 A，而四个选项中，只有 D 选项提到了融化，符合逻辑关系，A、B、C 三个选项都不符合。

Question 21

A. NO CHANGE

B. itself,

C. itself, with damage and

D. itself possibly,

1. 答案

B。

2. 精讲

简洁性题。题目所在句的问题是 repeat 和 again 两个词重复，删掉 again 即可得到正确答案，所以选择 B 选项。A 选项是错误的；C 选项虽然删掉了 again，但是 damage 和 harmful effects 两词又出现重复，所以错误；D 选项中的 possibly 和 may 出现重复，所以错误。

> **Question 22**
>
> To make this paragraph most logical, sentence 4 should be placed
>
> A. where it is now.
>
> B. after sentence 1.
>
> C. after sentence 2.
>
> D. after sentence 5.

1. 答案

D。

2. 精讲

逻辑顺序题。先来判断插入句的逻辑，sentence 4 这句话中存在 "this + n." 形式，可以判断这是一个指代逻辑，相应地预判出其前一句话一定会提及一种 crucial information。首先我们来看 A 选项，把它放在第 3 句话的后面，第 3 句话讲的是 Box 在 2012 年观察到的模式可能会重复出现，对极地的生态系统有害，所以第 3 句主要在讲一种模式，而不是信息，所以错误；B 选项是放在第 1 句之后，第 1 句讲的是 Box 的研究很重要，因为 2012 年的大火可能不是一次性的现象，这也不是一种重要信息，所以错误；C 选项是放在第 2 句之后，第 2 句说的是根据科学家的说法，上升的极地气温使得北纬地区植被更茂盛，并且更易发生火灾，这句话讲的是一种现象，不是一种信息，所以错误；D 选项是放在第 5 句之后，第 5 句讲的是对于 Box 和他的团队来说，下一步是去格陵兰进行取样，来确定 soot 能在多大程度上导致冰盖的融化，这就是 Box 想去获取的重要信息，所以 D 选项正确。

第七章

职业类文章真题精讲

Questions 23–33 are based on the following passage.

Coworking: A Creative Solution

When I left my office job as a website developer at a small company for a position that allowed me to work full-time from home, I thought I had it made: I gleefully traded in my suits and dress shoes for sweatpants and slippers, my frantic early-morning bagged lunch packing for a leisurely midday trip to my refrigerator. The novelty of this comfortable work-from-home life, however, [23] soon got worn off quickly. Within a month, I found myself feeling isolated despite having frequent email and instant messaging contact with my colleagues. Having become frustrated trying to solve difficult problems, [24] no colleagues were nearby to share ideas. It was during this time that I read an article [25] into coworking spaces.

23

A. NO CHANGE
B. was promptly worn
C. promptly wore
D. wore

24

A. NO CHANGE
B. colleagues were important for sharing ideas.
C. ideas couldn't be shared with colleagues.
D. I missed having colleagues nearby to consult.

25

A. NO CHANGE
B. about
C. upon
D. for

The article, published by *Forbes* magazine, explained that coworking spaces are designated locations that, for a fee, individuals can use to conduct their work. The spaces are usually stocked with standard office <u>26 equipment, such as photocopiers, printers, and fax machines. 27 In these locations, however,</u> the spaces often include small meeting areas and larger rooms for hosting presentations. 28 <u>The cost of launching a new coworking business in the United States is estimated to be approximately $58,000.</u>

26

A. NO CHANGE

B. equipment, such as:

C. equipment such as:

D. equipment, such as,

27

A. NO CHANGE

B. In addition to equipment,

C. For these reasons,

D. Likewise,

28

The writer is considering deleting the underlined sentence. Should the sentence be kept or deleted?

A. Kept, because it provides a detail that supports the main topic of the paragraph.

B. Kept, because it sets up the main topic of the paragraph that follows.

C. Deleted, because it blurs the paragraph's main focus with a loosely related detail.

D. Deleted, because it repeats information that has been provided in an earlier paragraph.

What most caught my interest, though, was a quotation from someone who described coworking spaces as "melting pots of creativity." The article refers to a 2012 survey in which **29** 64 percent of respondents noted that coworking spaces prevented them from completing tasks in a given time. The article goes on to suggest that the most valuable resources provided by coworking spaces are actually the people **30** whom use them.

29

At this point, the writer wants to add specific information that supports the main topic of the paragraph.

Perceived Effect of Coworking on Business Skills

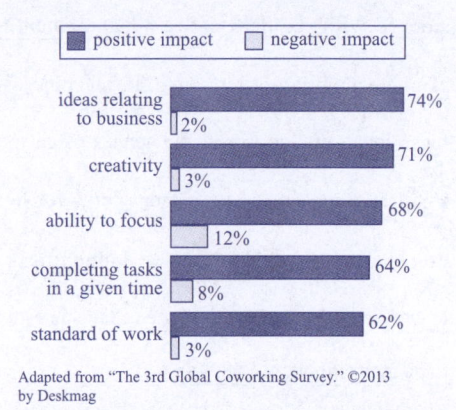

■ positive impact   □ negative impact

Category	Positive	Negative
ideas relating to business	74%	2%
creativity	71%	3%
ability to focus	68%	12%
completing tasks in a given time	64%	8%
standard of work	62%	3%

Adapted from "The 3rd Global Coworking Survey." ©2013 by Deskmag

Which choice most effectively completes the sentence with relevant and accurate information based on the graph above?

A. NO CHANGE
B. 71 percent of respondents indicated that using a coworking space increased their creativity.
C. respondents credited coworking spaces with giving them 74 percent of their ideas relating to business.
D. respondents revealed that their ability to focus on their work improved by 12 percent in a coworking space.

30

A. NO CHANGE
B. whom uses
C. who uses
D. who use

[1] Thus, even though I already had all the equipment I needed in my home office, I decided to try using a coworking space in my city. [2] Because I was specifically interested in coworking's reported benefits related to creativity, I chose a facility that offered a bright, open work area where I wouldn't be isolated. [3] Throughout the morning, more people appeared. [4] Periods of quiet, during which everyone worked independently, were broken up occasionally with lively conversation. **31**

I liked the experience so much that I now go to the coworking space a few times a week. Over time, I've gotten to know several of my coworking **32** colleagues: another website developer, a graphic designer, a freelance writer, and several mobile app coders. Even those of us who work in disparate fields are able to **33** share advice and help each other brainstorm. In fact, it's the diversity of their talents and experiences that makes my coworking colleagues so valuable.

31

The writer wants to add the following sentence to the paragraph.

After filling out a simple registration form and taking a quick tour of the facility, I took a seat at a table and got right to work on my laptop.

The best placement for the sentence is immediately

A. before sentence 1.

B. after sentence 1.

C. after sentence 2.

D. after sentence 3.

32

A. NO CHANGE

B. colleagues;

C. colleagues,

D. colleagues

33

A. NO CHANGE

B. give some wisdom

C. proclaim our opinions

D. opine

真经派精讲

Question 23

A. NO CHANGE

B. was promptly worn

C. promptly wore

D. wore

1. 答案

D。

2. 精讲

简洁性题。原句问题是 soon 和 quickly 意思重复，需要删掉一个，所以 A 错误；B 选项和 C 选项的问题是 promptly 和 quickly 词义重复，所以错误；D 选项没有重复性问题，另外，因为作者在叙述一件过去发生的事情，所以需要用过去时，时态也非常正确。

Question 24

A. NO CHANGE

B. colleagues were important for sharing ideas.

C. ideas couldn't be shared with colleagues.

D. I missed having colleagues nearby to consult.

1. 答案

D。

2. 精讲

悬垂修饰语。这道题出现了考查悬垂修饰语的八大句型之一的伴随状语结构，Having become frustrated trying to solve difficult problems 引导了伴随状语，no colleagues were nearby to share ideas 是主句部分，这时我们就要想到伴随状语的主语和主句主语的一致性原则，看主句主语是否能发出伴随状语的动作，这句话主句的主语是 no colleagues（没有同事），伴随状语的动作是 having become frustrated（感觉到挫败），从句意来看，作者是在叙述自己的经历，由于在家里工作，周围没有同事，所以感觉到很孤独，而且也很难解决困难的问题，所以主句主语应该是第一人称 I，那么只有 D 选项符合要求，A、B、C 选项的主语都是错误的。

Question 25

A. NO CHANGE

B. about

C. upon

D. for

1. 答案

B。

2. 精讲

标准搭配题。标准搭配题主要考查名词和介词、形容词和介词还有动词和介词的搭配，这道题考的是名词 article 和介词的搭配，想表达一篇文章是关于某个主题的意思，应该用介词 about，A 选项 into 是"在……里面"的意思，C 选项 upon 和 on 有同样的意思，表示"在……上面"，D 选项 for 表示对象或目的，所以 A、C、D 选项都不对。

Question 26

A. NO CHANGE

B. equipment, such as:

C. equipment such as:

D. equipment, such as,

1. 答案

A。

2. 精讲

多余符号题。这句话考查的是举例引导词 such as 的符号用法，正确的用法应该是"S + V + O, such as A, B and C. "，所以 A 选项正确；B、C 选项都在 such as 后加了一个多余的冒号，错误；D 选项在 such as 后加上了多余的逗号，错误。

Question 27

A. NO CHANGE

B. In addition to equipment,

C. For these reasons,

D. Likewise,

1. 答案

B。

2. 精讲

开篇句 & 结论句 & 过渡句题。这道题需要我们在两句中间加一个过渡逻辑词，我们先把两句话的意思理解一下。前一句的意思是：这些空间里储存了标准的办公设备，比如复印机、打印机和传真机；后一句的意思是：这些空间包含小的会议区和用于组织发布会的大房间。这两句话的主语都是spaces，而且分别说了spaces里有什么东西，应该是一种并列关系，因此B选项正确，in addition to 的意思是"除了……，还有……"，是并列逻辑词；A选项是转折逻辑，但前后两句中没有对比反义词，错误；C选项是因果逻辑，前后两句中不存在原因和解释，错误；D选项 likewise 意思是"一样的是"，是比较逻辑，表明前后两句表达的是同样的情况，为了说明同样的观点，不符合句意，错误。

Question 28

The writer is considering deleting the underlined sentence. Should the sentence be kept or deleted?

A. Kept, because it provides a detail that supports the main topic of the paragraph.

B. Kept, because it sets up the main topic of the paragraph that follows.

C. Deleted, because it blurs the paragraph's main focus with a loosely related detail.

D. Deleted, because it repeats information that has been provided in an earlier paragraph.

1. 答案

C。

2. 精讲

焦点题。保留还是删减一个句子要看这个句子与前后的句子之间是否有紧密的逻辑关系，若有，则须保留，若没有，即可删掉。画线句子的意思是"开启一个新的一起工作的商业模式的费用预计约为 58 000 美元"，而其前一句是在讲这些空间包含会议室和用于发布会的房间，两句话之间没有太强的关联性，所以判断这句话是可以删减的，A、B 选项即可排除。C、D 选项的正确性要通过选项删减的原因来判断，C 选项说的是因为这个句子用一个不相关的细节模糊了段落的主旨，这个句子确实与主旨无关，所以正确。D 选项说的是因为这句话重复了前一段提到的信息，不符合原文，所以错误。

Question 29

At this point, the writer wants to add specific information that supports the main topic of the paragraph. Which choice most effectively completes the sentence with relevant and accurate information based on the graph above?

A. NO CHANGE

B. 71 percent of respondents indicated that using a coworking space increased their creativity.

C. Respondents credited coworking spaces with giving them 74 percent of their ideas relating to businesss.

D. Respondents revealed that their ability to focus on their work improved by 12 percent in a coworking space.

1. 答案

B。

2. 精讲

数据信息题。数据信息题的正确答案要符合两个要求，一要符合题干要求，二要符合图表信息。本题题干要求添加一个具体信息支持段落观点，本段观点句是第一句，该句句意是：引起我兴趣的是某个人的一句话把共同工作空间描述成"创新的熔炉"。根据观点句，我们预测下一句的细节信息应该围绕创新来讲述。A 选项的核心是在规定的时间完成相应的任务，不符合，错误；B 选项的核心是创新，符合题干要求，再看其是否符合图表信息，选项说 71% 的受访者表明共同工作空间可以提升他们的创造力，符合图表的信息，所以正确；C 选项的核心是与商业相关的想法，不符合题干，错误；D 选项的核心是聚焦工作的能力，不符合题干要求，错误。

Question 30

A. NO CHANGE

B. whom uses

C. who uses

D. who use

1. 答案

D。

2. 精讲

一致性题。这道题涉及两个考点，一个是主谓一致原则，一个是定语从句引导词的选择。动词 use 应该与 people 主谓一致，所以排除 B、C 选项；另外 who 和 whom 都可以引导定语从句来修饰人，但是 who 在从句中作主语，而 whom 在从句中作宾语，在本句中引导词后是 use them，说明缺少主语，那么引导词要在从句中充当主语，所以要用 who 引导，选择 D 选项。

Question 31

The writer wants to add the following sentence to the paragraph.

After filling out a simple registration form and taking a quick tour of the facility, I took a seat at a table and got right to work on my laptop.

The best placement for the sentence is immediately

A. before sentence 1.

B. after sentence 1.

C. after sentence 2.

D. after sentence 3.

1. 答案

C。

2. 精讲

逻辑顺序题。先判断插入句的逻辑，本句中出现了 the facility，判断其为指代逻辑，即前一句要提及 facility。四个选项涉及 sentence 1、sentence 2 和 sentence 3，看原文只有 sentence 2 提及了 facility，所以插入句应该放在 sentence 2 的后面，选择 C 选项，在这句话中 facility 的意思是"场所；地点"。

注：facility [fə'sɪləti] n. 场所；地点

= equipment 设备

= talent 天赋

第七章 职业类文章真题精讲

> **Question 32**
>
> A. NO CHANGE
>
> B. colleagues;
>
> C. colleagues,
>
> D. colleagues

1. 答案

A。

2. 精讲

句中符号题。根据句意，我们确定此题考查的是同位语的符号，another website developer、a graphic designer、a freelance writer 和 several mobile app coders 都是在具体解释 colleagues，同位语符号有逗号、冒号和破折号三种，所以先排除 B、D 选项。C 选项的 colleagues 后面使用了逗号，可以引导同位语，但是逗号放在这里会产生歧义，会让读者误认为 colleagues 一词和后面的词是并列关系，所以错误。

> **Question 33**
>
> A. NO CHANGE
>
> B. give some wisdom
>
> C. proclaim our opinions
>
> D. opine

1. 答案

A。

2. 精讲

风格 & 语气题。此类型题目的正确选项必须符合两个要求，一是选项的表达必须是标准的英语表达，不能太口语化，二是选项要符合段落主题。画线部分所在句的意思是：那些工作在不同领域的我们可以_____并且帮助彼此集思广益。A 选项的语意符合原文，通过分享建议来帮助彼此集思广益；B 选项的表达太口语化，所以错误；C、D 选项都是表达意见，语意不符。

注：**opine** [əʊˈpaɪn] *v.* 表达

proclaim [prəˈkleɪm] *v.* 声明

第八章

人文学科类文章真题精讲

Questions 34-44 are based on the following passage.

The Consolations of Philosophy

Long viewed by many as the stereotypical useless major, philosophy is now being seen by many students and prospective employers as in fact a very useful and practical major, offering students a host of transferable skills with relevance to the modern workplace. [34] In broad terms, philosophy is the study of meaning and the values underlying thought and behavior. But [35] more pragmatically, the discipline encourages students to analyze complex material, question conventional beliefs, and express thoughts in a concise manner.

34

A. NO CHANGE
B. For example,
C. In contrast,
D. Nevertheless,

35

A. NO CHANGE
B. speaking in a more pragmatic way,
C. speaking in a way more pragmatically,
D. in a more pragmatic-speaking way,

Because philosophy **36** teaching students not what to think but how to think, the age-old discipline offers consistently useful tools for academic and professional achievement. **37** A 1994 survey concluded that only 18 percent of American colleges required at least one philosophy course. **38** Therefore, between 1992 and 1996, more than 400 independent philosophy departments were eliminated from institutions.

36

A. NO CHANGE
B. teaches
C. to teach
D. and teaching

37

Which choice most effectively sets up the information that follows?

A. Consequently, philosophy students have been receiving an increasing number of job offers.
B. Therefore, because of the evidence, colleges increased their offerings in philosophy.
C. Notwithstanding the attractiveness of this course of study, students have resisted majoring in philosophy.
D. However, despite its many utilitarian benefits, colleges have not always supported the study of philosophy.

38

A. NO CHANGE
B. Thus,
C. Moreover,
D. However,

More recently, colleges have recognized the practicality and increasing popularity of studying philosophy and have markedly increased the number of philosophy programs offered. By 2008 there were 817 programs, up from 765 a decade before. In addition, the number of four-year graduates in philosophy has grown 46 percent in a decade. Also, studies have found that those students who major in philosophy often do better than students from other majors in both verbal reasoning and analytical [39] writing. These results can be measured by standardized test scores. On the Graduate Record Examination (GRE), for example, students intending to study philosophy in graduate school [40] has scored higher than students in all but four other majors.

These days, many [41] student's majoring in philosophy have no intention of becoming philosophers; instead they plan to apply those skills to other disciplines. Law and business specifically benefit from the complicated theoretical issues raised in the study of philosophy, but philosophy can be just as useful in engineering or any field requiring complex analytic skills.

39

Which choice most effectively combines the sentences at the underlined portion?

A. writing as

B. writing, and these results can be

C. writing, which can also be

D. writing when the results are

40

A. NO CHANGE

B. have scored

C. scores

D. scoring

41

A. NO CHANGE

B. students majoring

C. students major

D. student's majors

42 That these skills are transferable across professions **43** which makes them especially beneficial to twenty-first-century students. Because today's students can expect to hold multiple jobs—some of which may not even exist yet—during **44** our lifetime, studying philosophy allows them to be flexible and adaptable.

High demand, advanced exam scores, and varied professional skills all argue for maintaining and enhancing philosophy courses and majors within academic institutions.

42

At this point, the writer is considering adding the following sentence.

The ancient Greek philosopher Plato, for example, wrote many of his works in the form of dialogues.

Should the writer make this addition here?

A. Yes, because it reinforces the passage's main point about the employability of philosophy majors.

B. Yes, because it acknowledges a common counterargument to the passage's central claim.

C. No, because it blurs the paragraph's focus by introducing a new idea that goes unexplained.

D. No, because it undermines the passage's claim about the employability of philosophy majors.

43

A. NO CHANGE
B. that
C. and
D. DELETE the underlined portion.

44

A. NO CHANGE
B. one's
C. his or her
D. their

★ 真经派精讲

Question 34

A. NO CHANGE

B. For example,

C. In contrast,

D. Nevertheless,

1. 答案

A。

2. 精讲

开篇句 & 结论句 & 过渡句题。这道题需要我们在两句间加一个过渡逻辑词，那么就要理解前后两句话的语意。前一句的意思是：哲学在很长时间内被认为是一个模式化的、无用的学科，但现在却被很多学生和未来的雇主认为是一个有用和实际的专业，能提供给学生很多可以用于工作中的技能；后一句说哲学是在研究思想和行为背后的意义和价值。这两句话之间并无直接的关系，所以判断逻辑比较困难，我们再看后面一句，其意思是：更务实一点说，这个学科鼓励学生分析复杂的资料、质疑传统的信仰，并且以一种简单的方式表达思想。我们发现这句话中存在转折逻辑词 but，说明前后句是对比关系，所以 A 选项符合句意，前一句是宽泛地说，后一句是务实地说，是宽泛和具体的对比，所以正确；B 选项是举例逻辑，表明本句话在对前一句进行解释，而这两句话之间没有直接的关系，错误；C、D 选项都是对比逻辑，和 B 选项的错误一致。

注：**stereotypical** [ˌsterɪəˈtɪpɪkl] *adj.* 模式化的

prospective [prəˈspektɪv] *adj.* 即将发生的；未来的

pragmatically [præɡˈmætɪklɪ] *adv.* 务实地

discipline [ˈdɪsəplɪn] *n.* 学科

> **Question 35**
>
> A. NO CHANGE
>
> B. speaking in a more pragmatic way,
>
> C. speaking in a way more pragmatically,
>
> D. in a more pragmatic-speaking way,

1. 答案

A。

2. 精讲

简洁性题。这道题考查表达的简洁性，A、B、C、D 四个选项表达的意思都一样，语法上也没有错误，但 A 选项最为简洁，用一个副词即可表达语意，根据简洁性原则，单词＞词组＞句子，所以 A 选项正确。

> **Question 36**
>
> A. NO CHANGE
>
> B. teaches
>
> C. to teach
>
> D. and teaching

1. 答案

B。

2. 精讲

句子边界题。这道题考查句子的完整性。because 引导原因状语从句，从句中主谓宾成分应该完整，A、C 选项在 philosophy 后面跟 teaching 或 to teach，即用非谓语动词作定语修饰 philosophy，导致原因状语从句中缺少谓语，所以错误；D 选项犯了两个错误，第一个是缺少谓语，第二个是 and 前后不平行，所以错误；B 选项 teaches 可以作谓语，解决句子不完整的问题，并且也符合主谓一致和时态一致的原则，所以正确。

Question 37

Which choice most effectively sets up the information that follows?

A. Consequently, philosophy students have been receiving an increasing number of job offers.

B. Therefore, because of the evidence, colleges increased their offerings in philosophy.

C. Notwithstanding the attractiveness of this course of study, students have resisted majoring in philosophy.

D. However, despite its many utilitarian benefits, colleges have not always supported the study of philosophy.

---

1. 答案

D。

2. 精讲

主旨题。此题要求加一个总说句，所以我们看一下后面一句话中的例子，以此推测总说句内容。后一句意思是"1994 年的调查表明只有 18% 的美国大学要求学生至少修一门哲学课"，说明那时的大学还不是很重视哲学课，所以总说句的语意必须符合我们对该句的理解。A 选项意思是"因此，哲学专业的学生收到的工作 offers 不断增加"，此句与我们的预测无关，所以错误；B 选项意思是"因此，由于这一证据，大学增加了哲学课的供给"，正好与我们的预测相反，所以错误；C 选项的意思是"虽然哲学研究很有吸引力，但是学生们依然拒绝把哲学作为专业选择"，此句主要在讲学生的行为，而不是学校不重视，所以错误；D 选项的意思是"然而，尽管有许多实用的好处，学校并不总是支持哲学的学习"，这句话与我们的预测一致，正确。

注：**notwithstanding** [ˌnɑːtwɪθˈstændɪŋ] *prep.* 虽然（= despite = in spite of）

utilitarian [juːtɪlɪˈteriən] *adj.* 实用的

Question 38

A. NO CHANGE

B. Thus,

C. Moreover,

D. However,

---

1. 答案

C。

2. 精讲

开篇句 & 结论句 & 过渡句题。此题需要在两句之间加一个逻辑过渡词，那么我们要理解前后两句的意思。前一句的意思是"1994 年的一项调查表明只有 18% 的美国大学要求学生至少修一门哲学课"，后一句的意思是"在 1992 到 1996 年之间，超过 400 个独立的哲学院系被学校机构取消了"。这两句话都在说学校不是很重视哲学课程，所以两句话应该是并列的逻辑关系，C 选项 moreover 的意思是"此外"，并列逻辑，所以正确；A、B 选项都是因果逻辑，前后两句话不存在解释和被解释的关系，所以错误；D 选项是转折逻辑，而前后两句不存在对比关系，所以错误。

Question 39

Which choice most effectively combines the sentences at the underlined portion?

A. writing as

B. writing, and these results can be

C. writing, which can also be

D. writing when the results are

1. 答案

A。

2. 精讲

句法题。此题要求把两个句子有效地合并成一个句子，并且符合两个要求：第一，连接两句话的逻辑连接词必须正确；第二，合并后的句子必须简洁。我们来看两句话的意思，确定两句话的逻辑关系；前一句意思是"此外，研究发现那些哲学专业的学生要比其他专业的学生在语言推理和分析性写作方面做得更好"，后一句的意思是"这些结果可以通过标准测试测量出来"。从语意上看，两句话之间是承接的逻辑关系，A 选项即为正确答案，as measured by standardized test scores 意思是"正像通过标准测试测量的那样"；B、D 选项中的 results 存在指代问题，因为前一句讲的是研究的发现，并不是结果，所以排除；C 选项中的 which 属于空指，在 SAT 文法中 which 不能指代一句话和一件事，必须指代名词。

Question 40

A. NO CHANGE

B. have scored

C. scores

D. scoring

1. 答案

B。

2. 精讲

一致性题。此题考查主谓一致原则。本句主语是 students，intending to study philosophy in graduate school 是分词作后置定语修饰主语 students，可以删掉，后面的谓语单复数形式必须与 students 一致，所以 B 选项正确；A、C 选项都错在主谓不一致；D 选项把谓语变成 scoring，导致该句缺少谓语。

Question 41

A. NO CHANGE

B. students majoring

C. students major

D. student's majors

1. 答案

B。

2. 精讲

多余符号题。此题我们需要分析一下句子结构：从句意看，many students 是主语，majoring in philosophy 是分词作主语的后置定语，have 是谓语，no intention of becoming philosophers 是宾语，所以 B 选项正确。A 选项中的单引号是不必要的，所以错误；C 选项中的 major 和句中的 have 都是动词，导致句中出现了双谓语，所以错误；D 选项把 majors 变成主语，但 majors 不能发出"have no intention of becoming philosophers"的动作，不符合句意，所以错误。

Question 42

At this point, the writer is considering adding the following sentence.

The ancient Greek philosopher Plato, for example, wrote many of his works in the form of dialogues.

Should the writer make this addition here?

A. Yes, because it reinforces the passage's main point about the employability of philosophy majors.

B. Yes, because it acknowledges a common counterargument to the passage's central claim.

C. No, because it blurs the paragraph's focus by introducing a new idea that goes unexplained.

D. No, because it undermines the passage's claim about the employability of philosophy majors.

1. 答案

C。

2. 精讲

焦点题。此题要求判断句子是否可以加入段落中，是否添加句子要看此句是否符合段落主旨。我们先看段落主旨句，即段落首句，意思是"这些日子，许多哲学专业的学生没有成为哲学家的意图；相反，他们计划把这些技能应用于其他学科"。添加的句子意思是"比如，古希腊哲学家柏拉图以对话的方式写了很多作品"。此句与主旨句没有任何关联性，所以判断此句不应该添加，所以排除 A、B 选项；判断 C、D 选项是否正确要通过选项中提供的不添加的原因来确定。C 选项说原因是这个例子通过引进一个新的、没有被解释过的信息模糊了段落的主旨，表达出此句与主旨的无关联性，所以正确；D 选项说原因是这个例子削弱了段落关于哲学专业可利用性的说法，这个例子与哲学专业的可利用性没有任何关系，更谈不上削弱，所以是错误的。

Question 43

A. NO CHANGE

B. that

C. and

D. DELETE the underlined portion.

1. 答案

D。

2. 精讲

句子边界题。对于此类题我们要先分析句子结构，that these skills are transferable across professions 是 that 引导的主语从句，makes 是谓语动词，所以在 makes 前面不能加任何连接词，否则就会导致句子缺少谓语，因此排除 A、B、C 三个选项，选择 D 选项。

Question 44

A. NO CHANGE

B. one's

C. his or her

D. their

1. 答案

D。

2. 精讲

人称混淆题。此类题考查第一人称、第二人称和第三人称的混淆问题。在此题中，物主代词 our 应该指代前半句的 students，students 属于第三人称，所以应该用 their 指代，因此排除 A 选项；B 选项 one's 指代单数名词，所以错误；C 选项 his or her 指代单数不知性别的名词，所以错误；D 选项 their 可以指代 students，正确。